AUDIO ACCESS INCLUDED

CLASSICAL GUITAR SHEET MUSIC

By Bridget Mermikides

PLAYBACK+
Speed • Pitch • Balance • Loop

To access audio visit:
www.halleonard.com/mylibrary

Enter Code
2433-7524-6190-6766

ISBN 978-1-5400-3228-7

HAL•LEONARD®

Visit Hal Leonard Online at
www.halleonard.com

Contact us:
Hal Leonard
7777 West Bluemound Road
Milwaukee, WI 53213
Email: info@halleonard.com

In Europe, contact:
Hal Leonard Europe Limited
42 Wigmore Street
Marylebone, London, W1U 2RN
Email: info@halleonardeurope.com

In Australia, contact:
Hal Leonard Australia Pty. Ltd.
4 Lentara Court
Cheltenham, Victoria, 3192 Australia
Email: info@halleonard.com.au

CONTENTS

INTRODUCTION

Many thanks for purchasing this book. It is a great privilege and pleasure to present to you this wonderful music collected from a range of musical eras and styles. The classical guitar is a beautiful expressive instrument but its repertoire of playable but effective music should always be expanded, and this book – along with *The Classical Guitar Compendium* and the *Classical Guitar Anthology* – is my contribution to this cause.

Included here are 25 new arrangements from Baroque, Classical and Romantic composers. I have worked hard to capture the essence of these masterpieces, staying as true as possible to the original form and harmony while making them a pleasure to play and listen to. I have also included seven repertoire pieces that are beloved works from Renaissance lute composers, Tarrega and Barrios. There is a range of technical challenge here, so plenty for all levels of players to get to grips with over a number of months or years.

Included in this book is a download link to recordings of me playing all the pieces, and while I hope they are useful to hear, do remember that you should aim to make these your own, allowing you to express your personal musicality through this beautiful music and instrument.

Bridget

Aria - Goldberg variations BWV988

Johann Sebastian Bach
Arranged by Bridget Mermikides

Drop D tuning:
(low to high) D-A-D-G-B-E

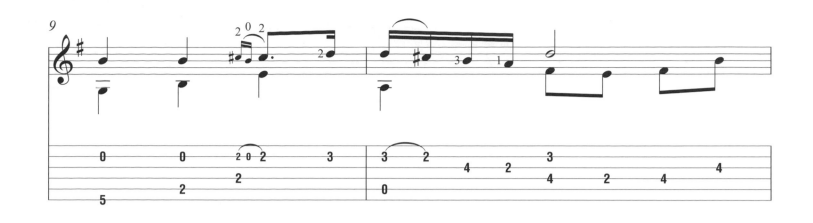

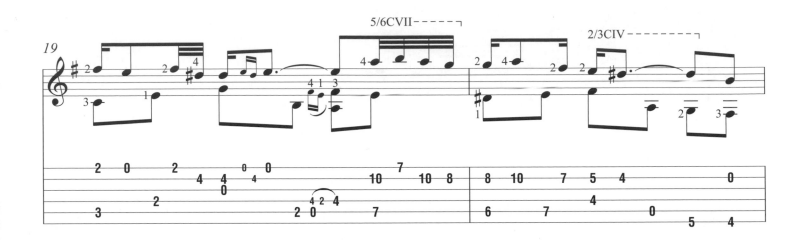

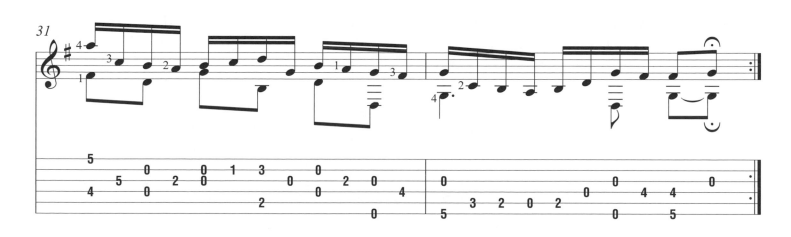

Toccata in D Minor

Johann Sebastian Bach
Arranged by Bridget Mermikides

Drop D tuning:
(low to high) D-A-D-G-B-E

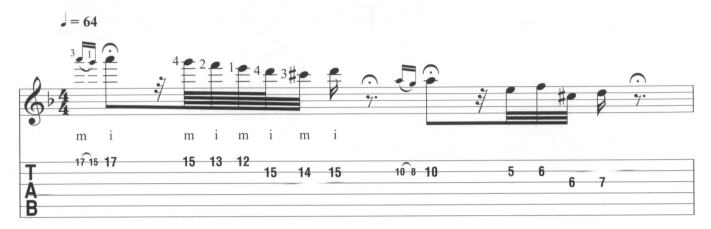

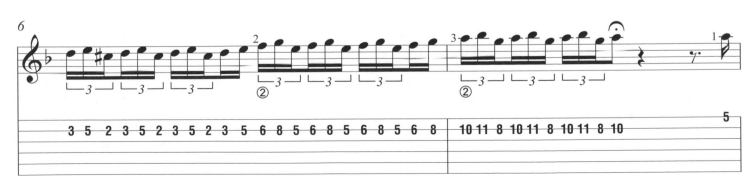

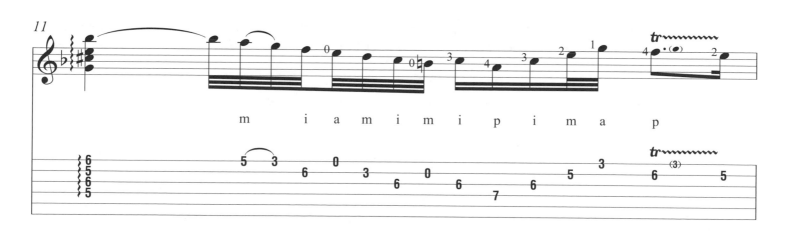

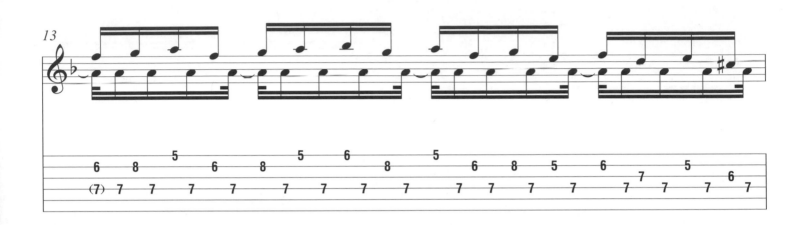

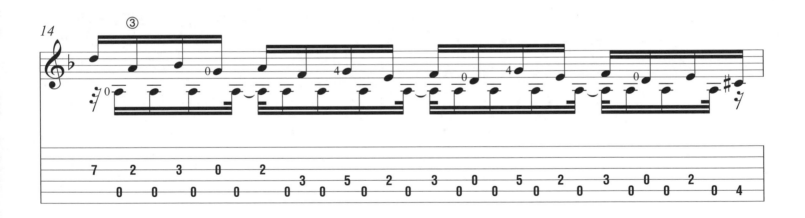

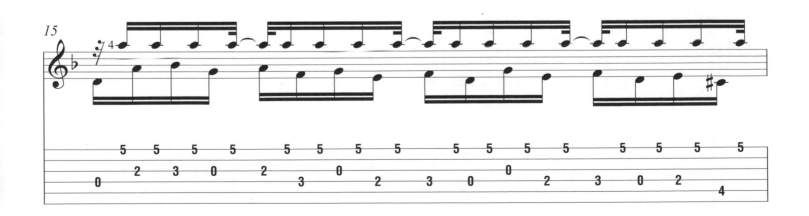

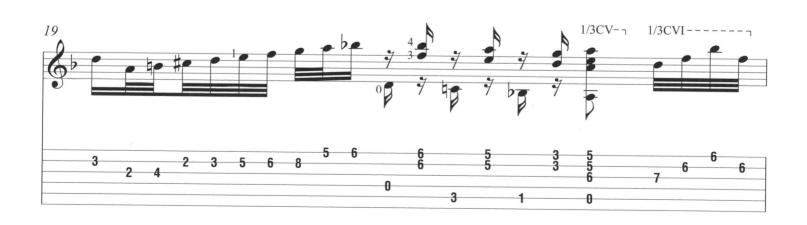

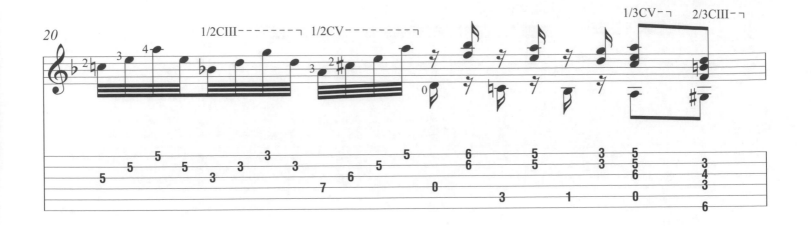

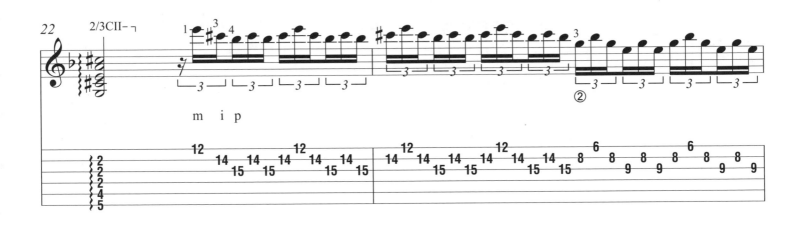

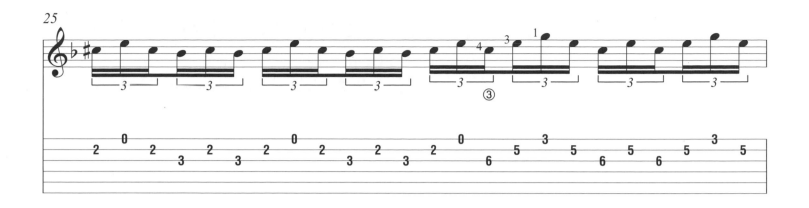

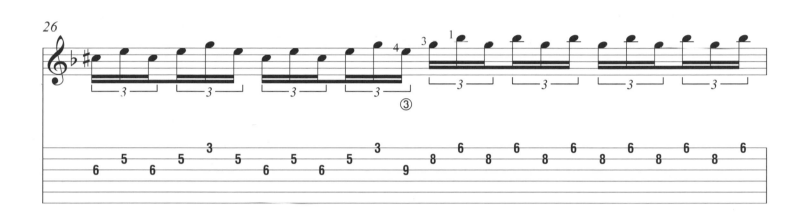

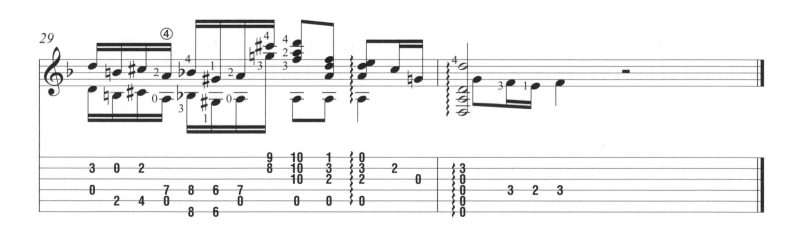

Una limosna por el amor de Dios

Augustine Barrios
Edited by Bridget Mermikides

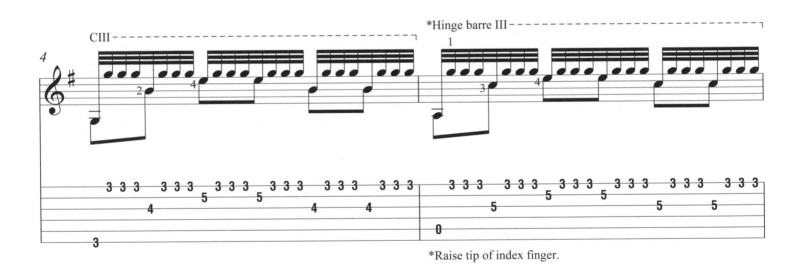

*Raise tip of index finger.

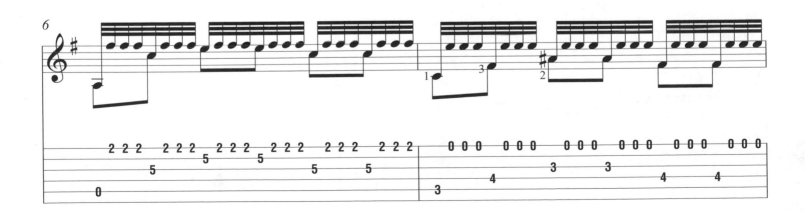

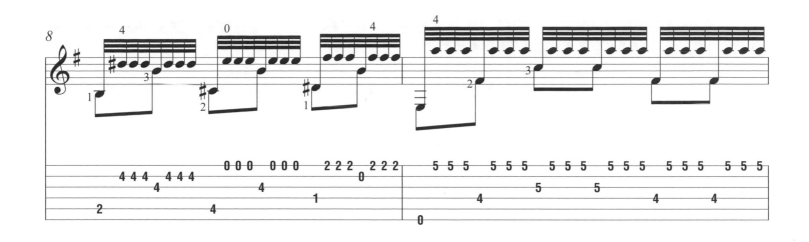

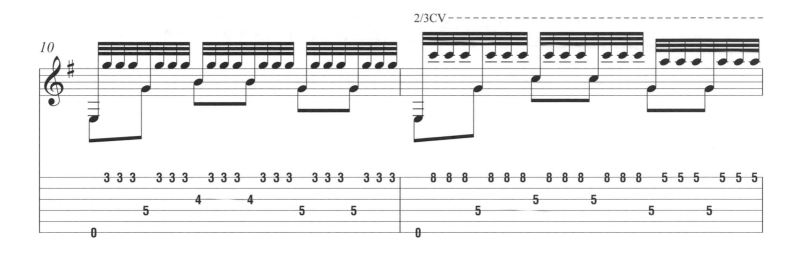

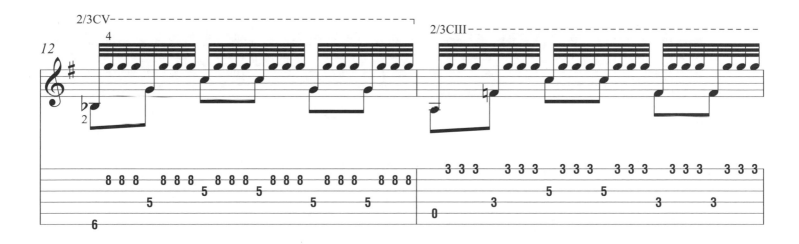

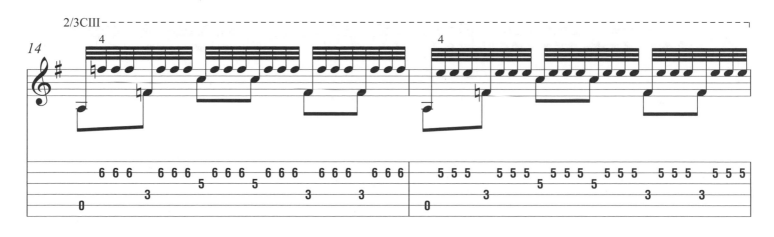

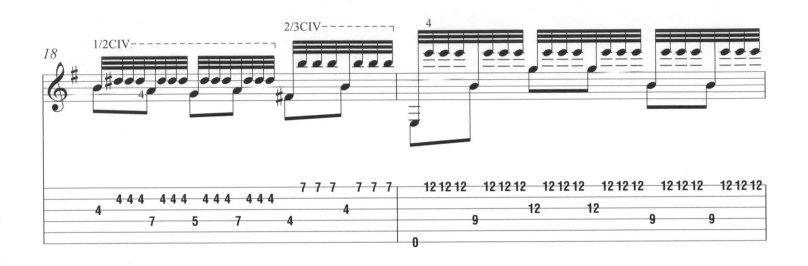

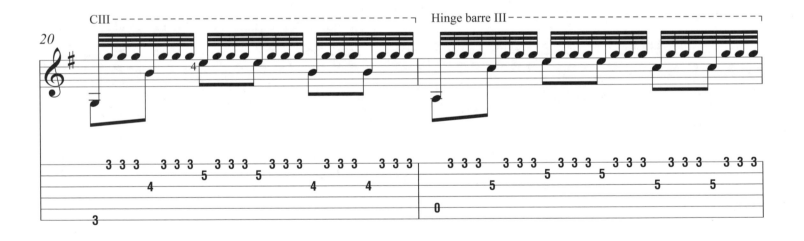

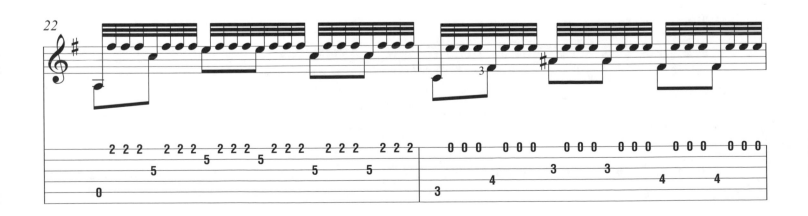

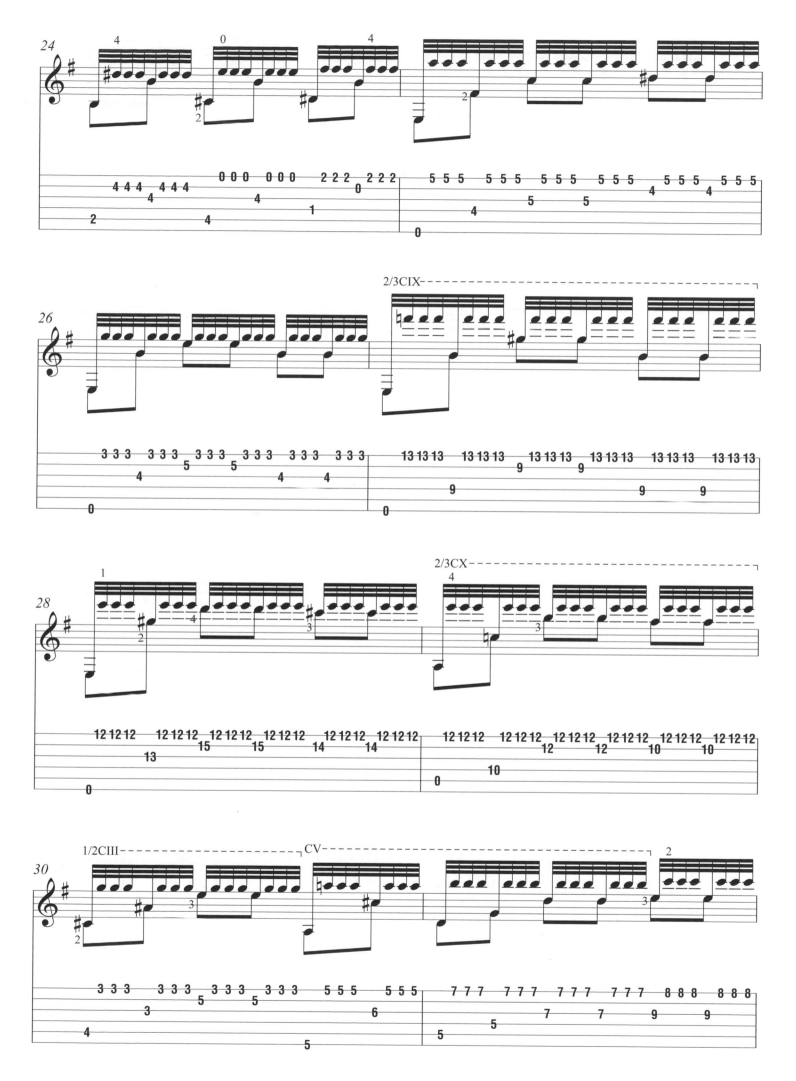

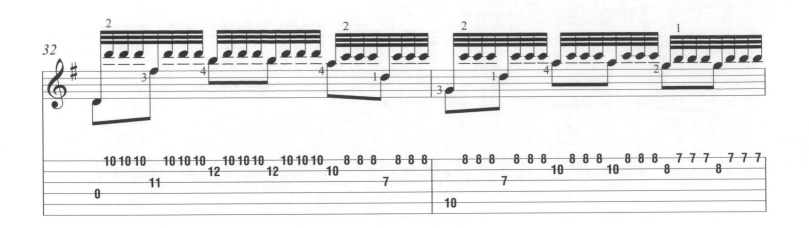

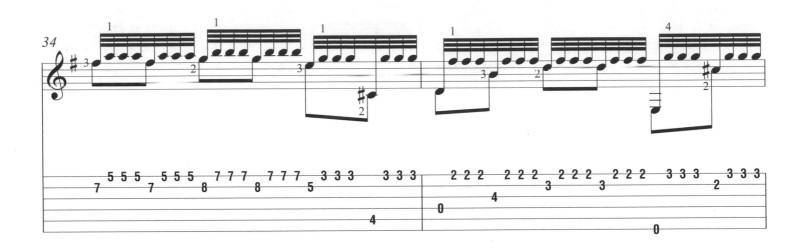

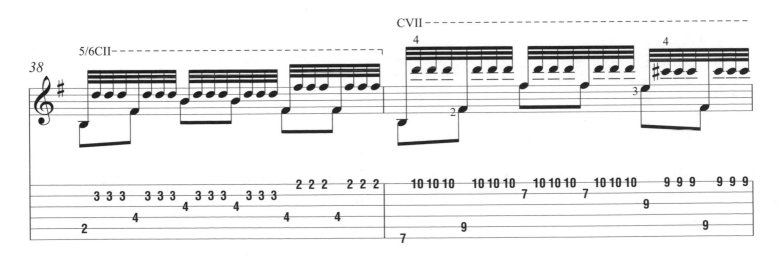

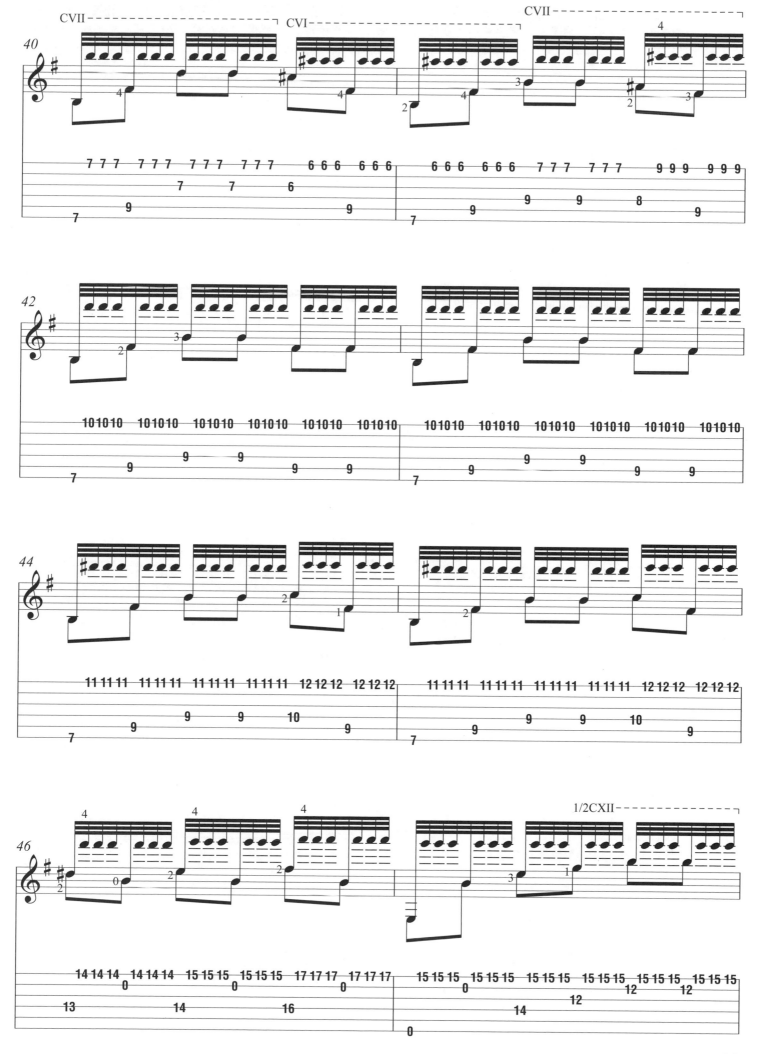

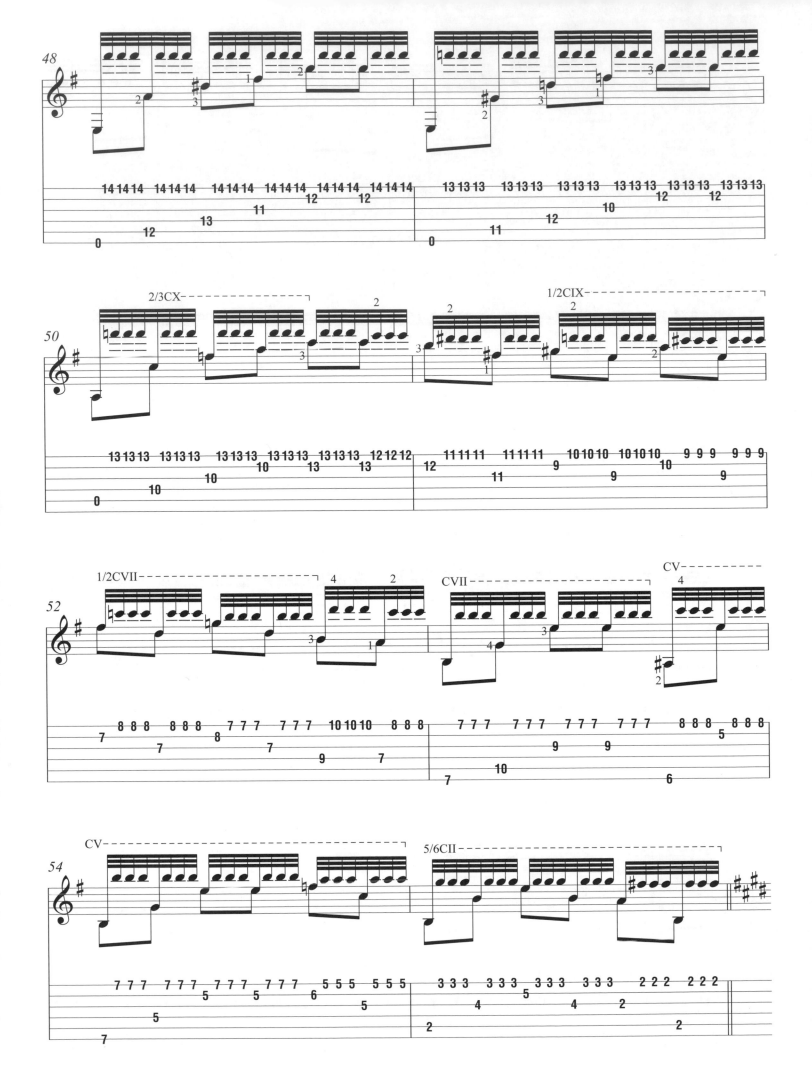

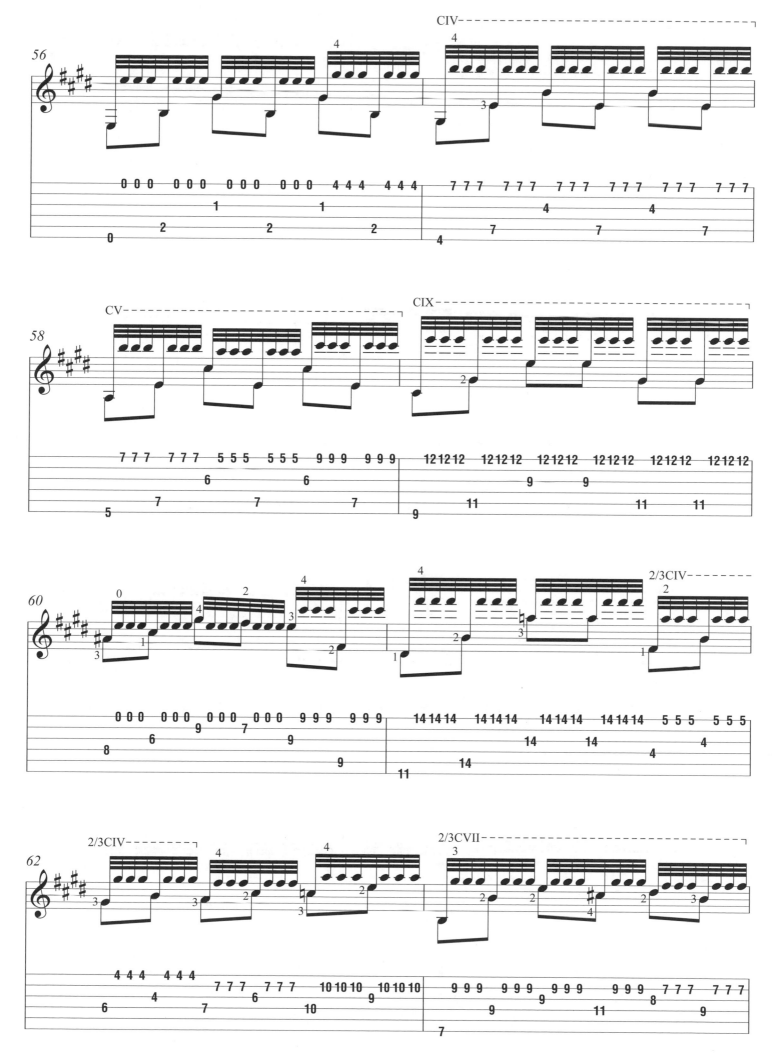

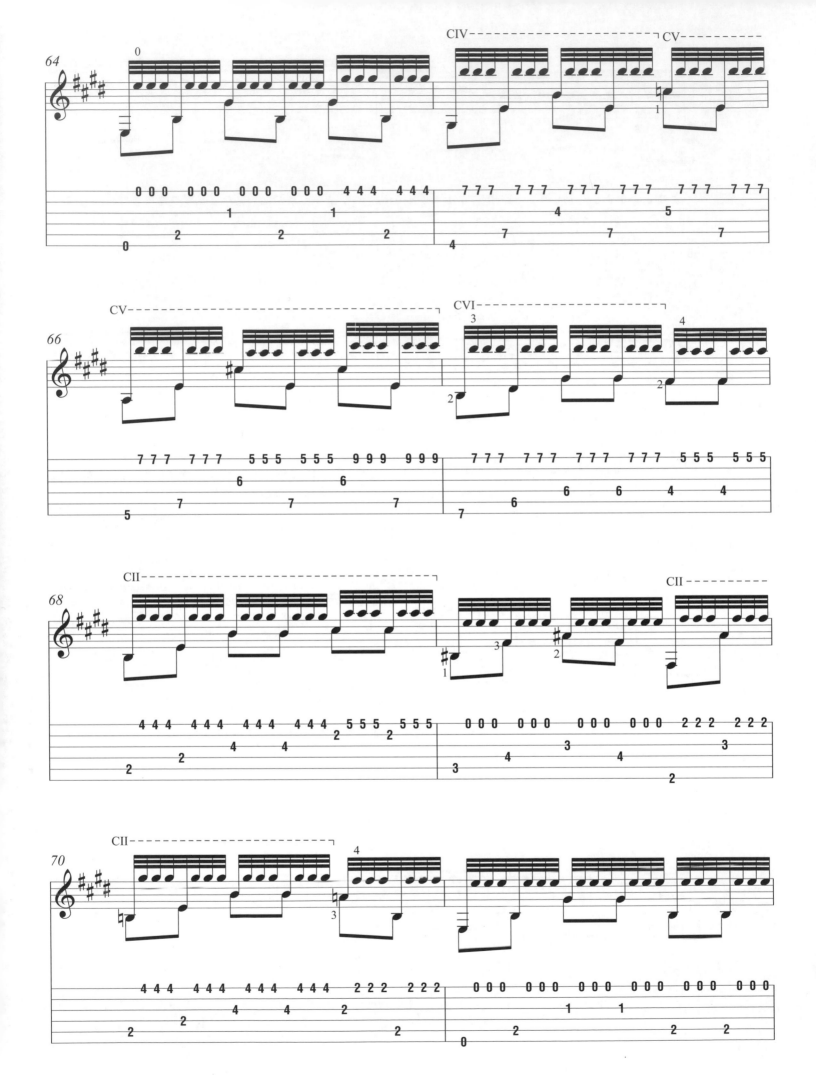

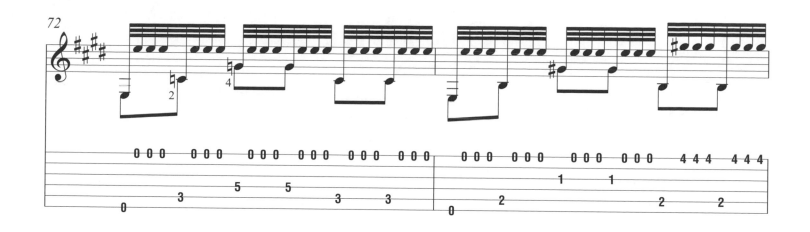

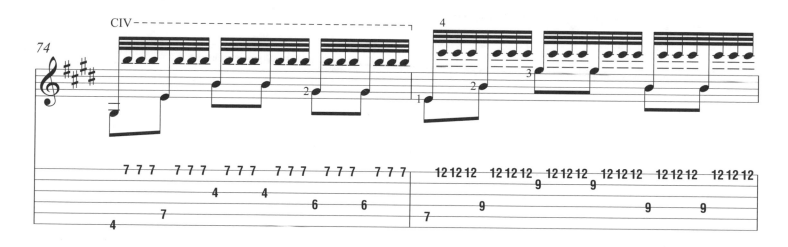

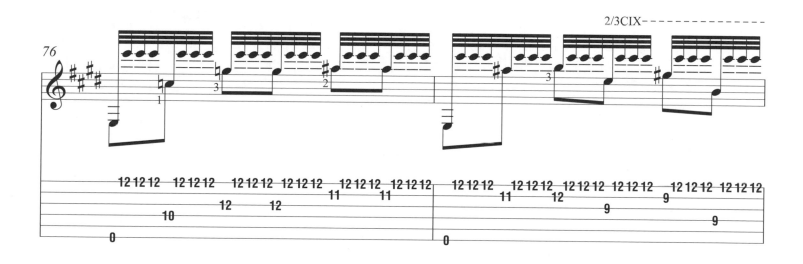

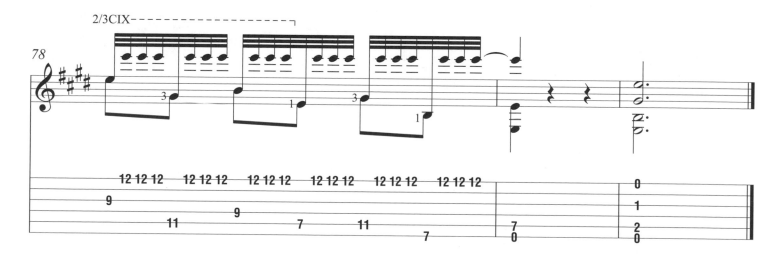

Casta Diva
From Norma

Vincenzo Bellini
Arranged by Bridget Mermikides

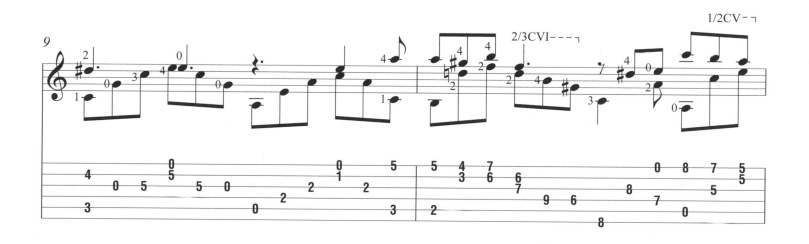

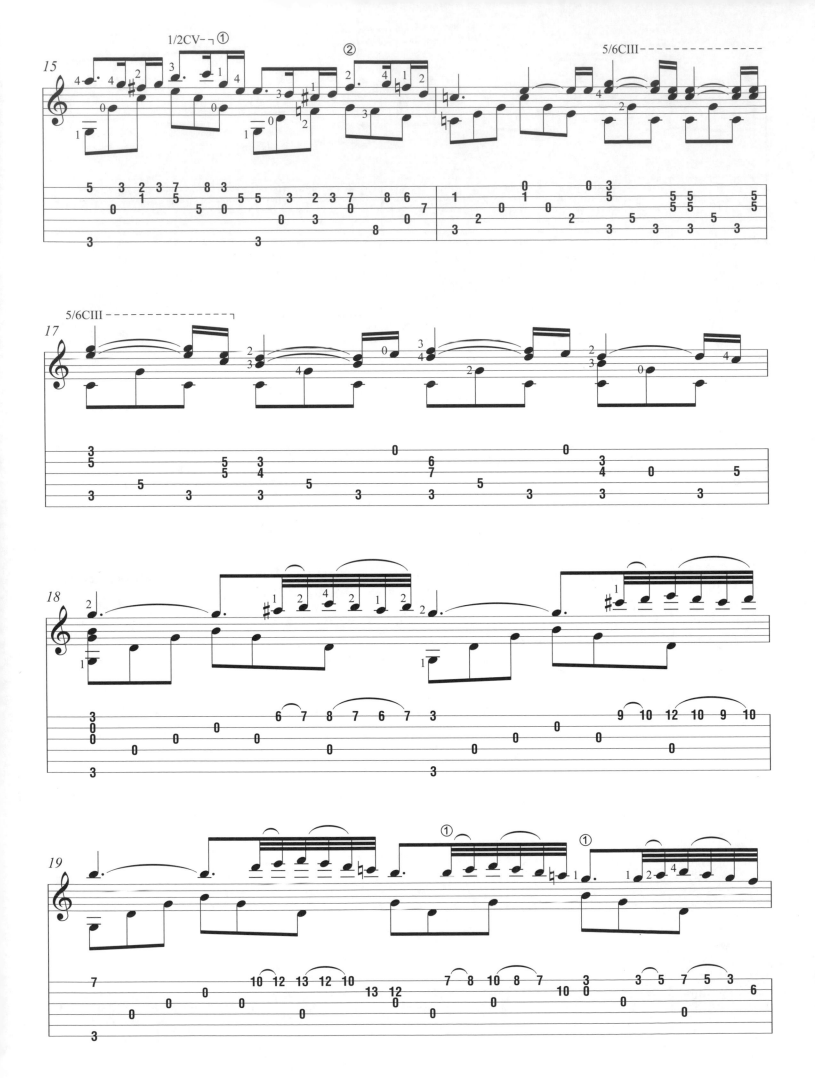

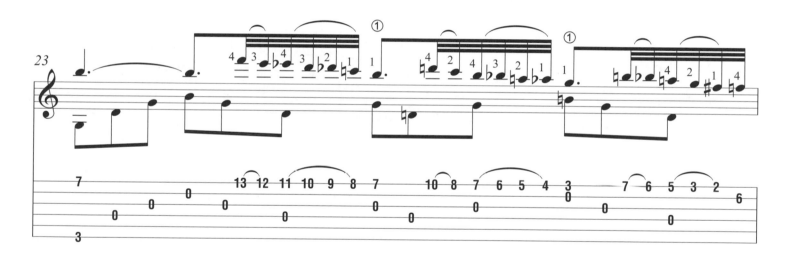

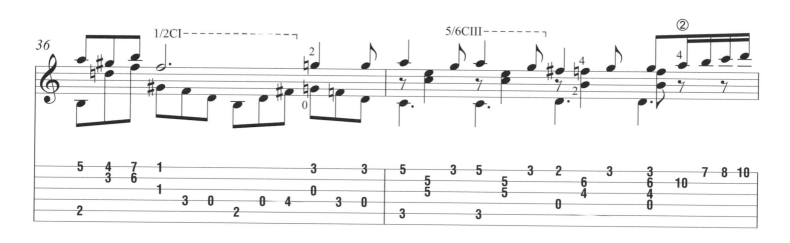

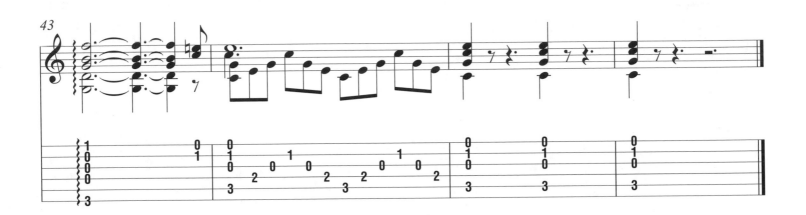

Fantasia no. 7

John Dowland
Edited by Bridget Mermikides

Tuning:
(low to high) E-A-D-F#-B-E

(Capo II optional)

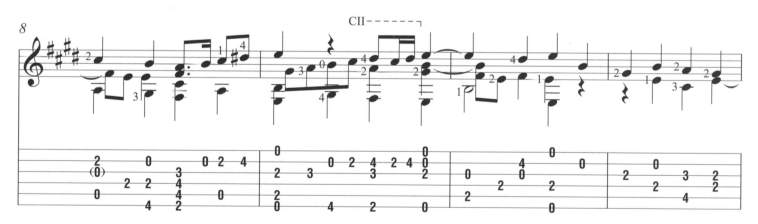

*Raise tip of index finger.

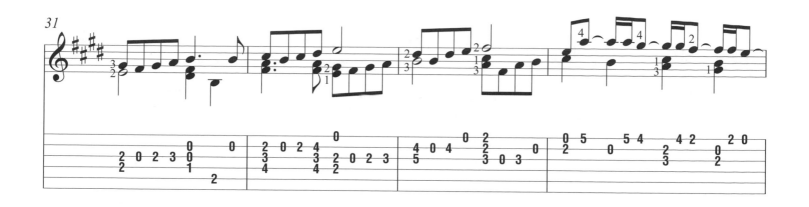

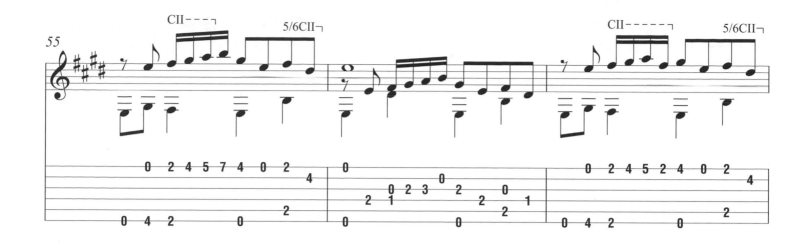

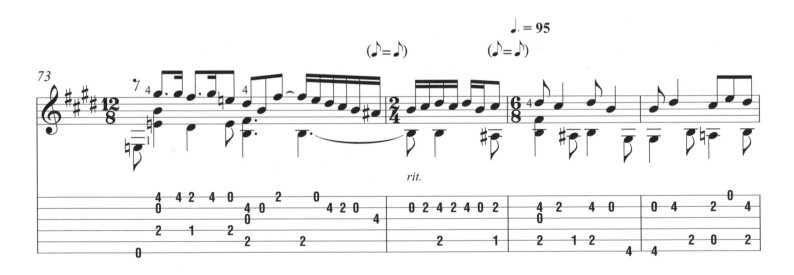

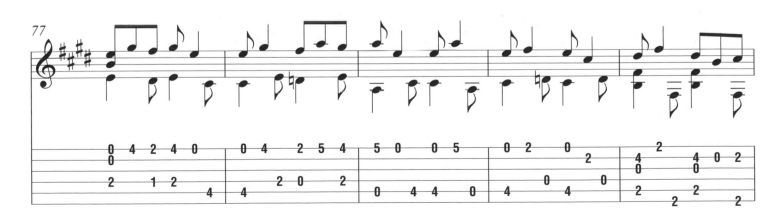

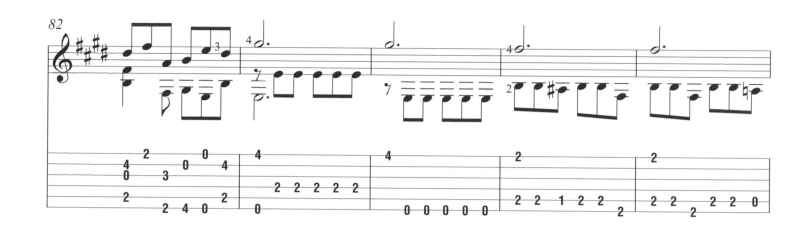

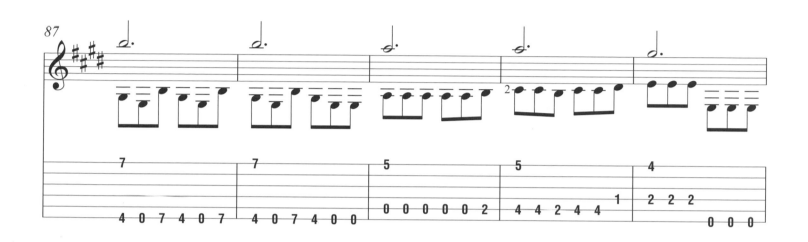

Land of Hope and Glory

Edward Elgar
Arranged by Bridget Mermikides

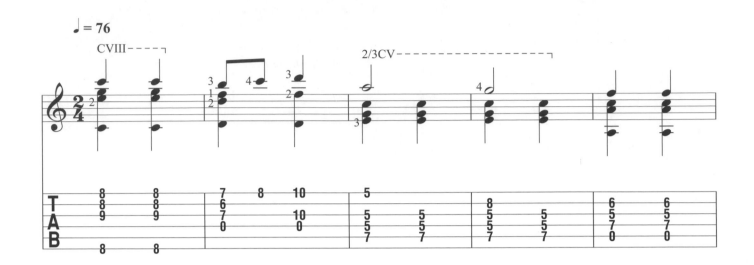

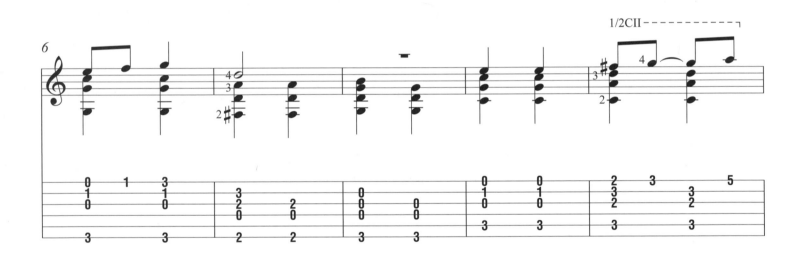

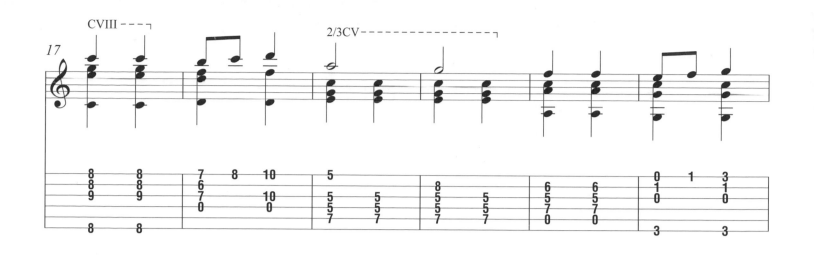

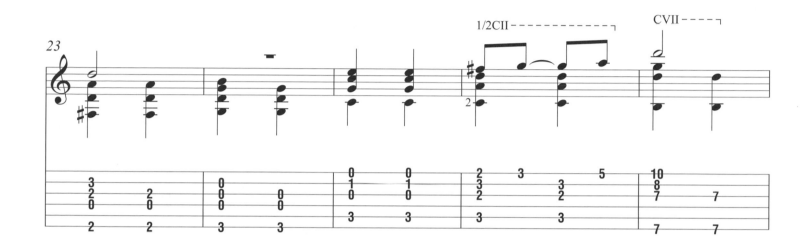

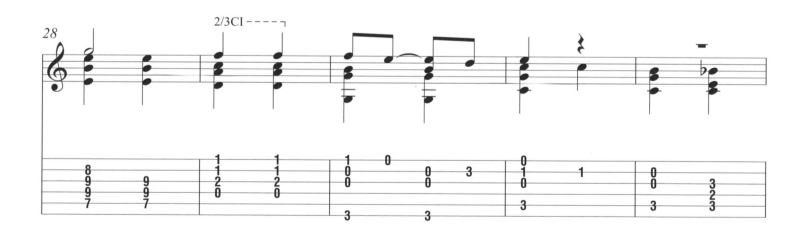

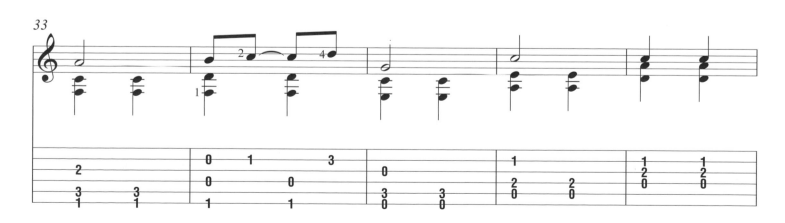

Salut d'Amour

Edward Elgar
Arranged by Bridget Mermikides

Drop D tuning:
(low to high) D-A-D-G-B-E

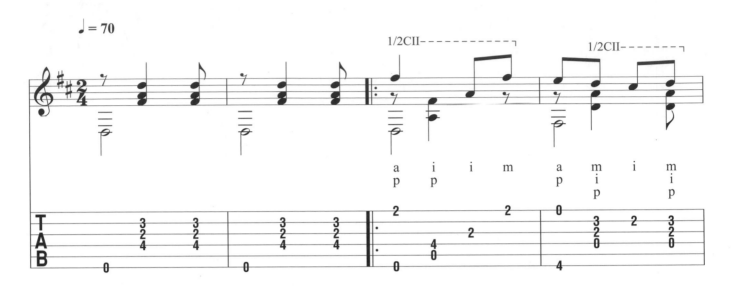

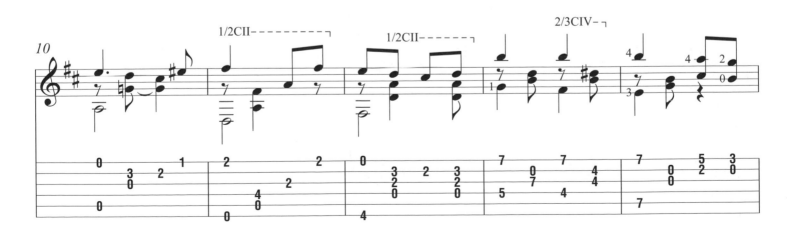

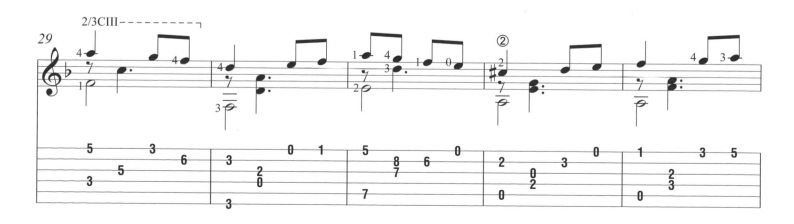

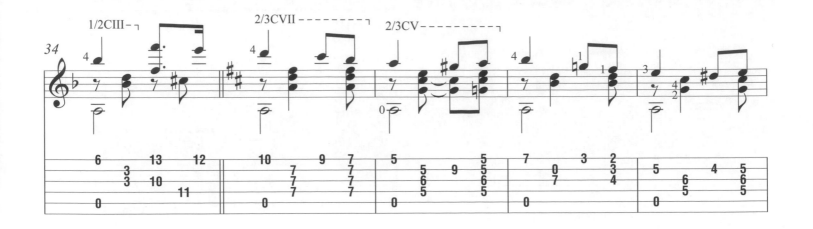

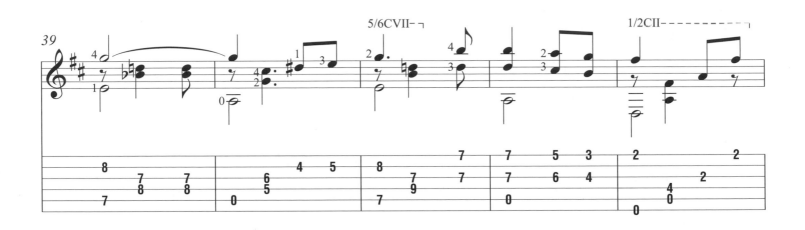

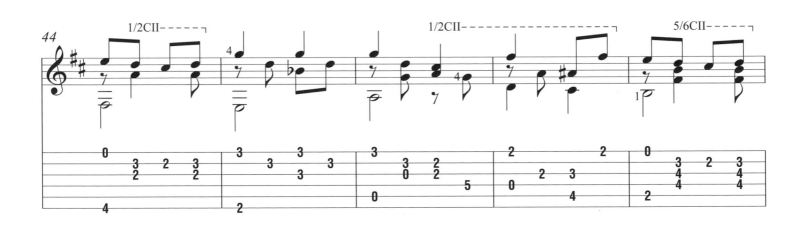

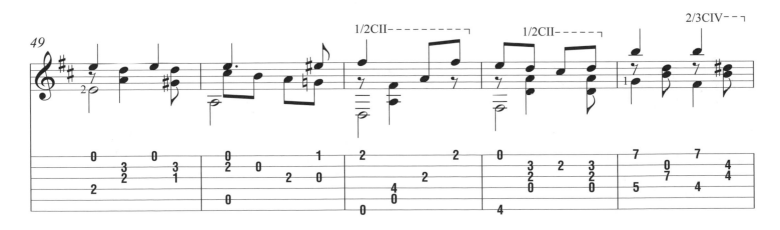

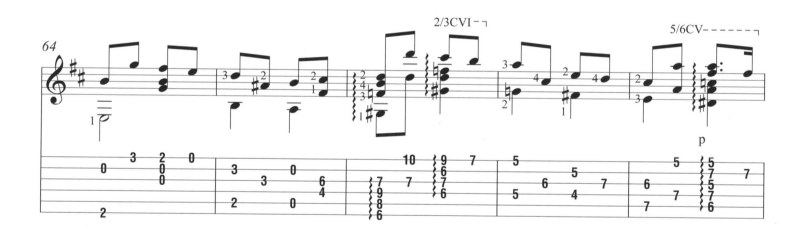

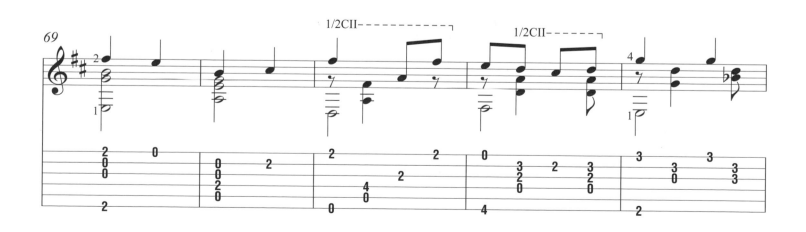

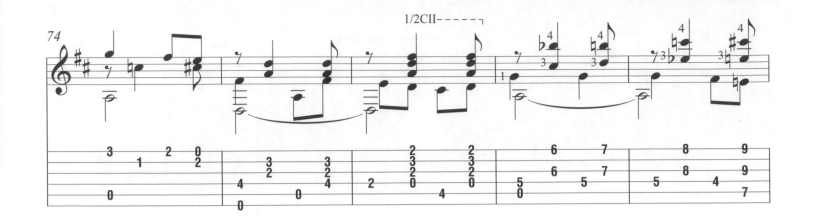

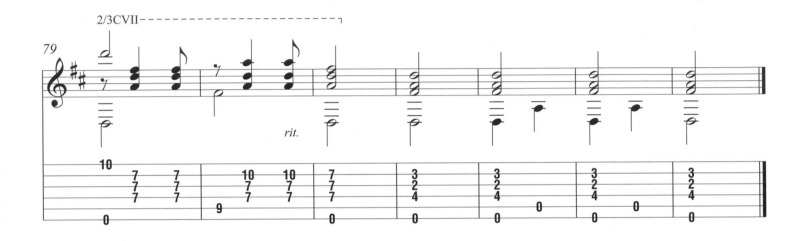

Wedding March

Felix Mendelssohn
Arranged by Bridget Mermikides

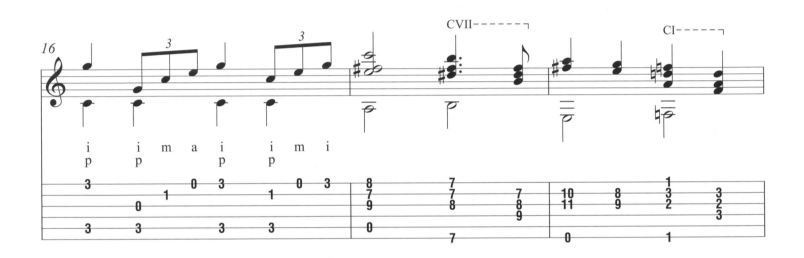

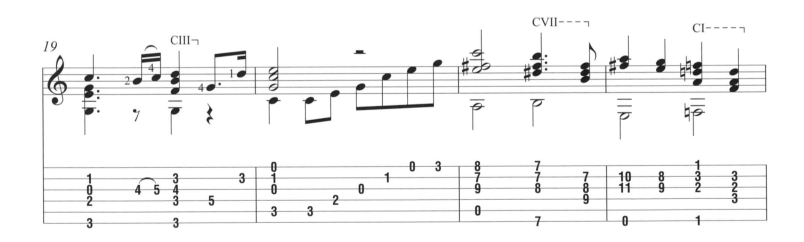

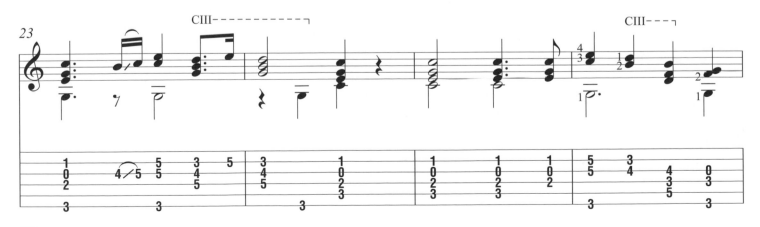

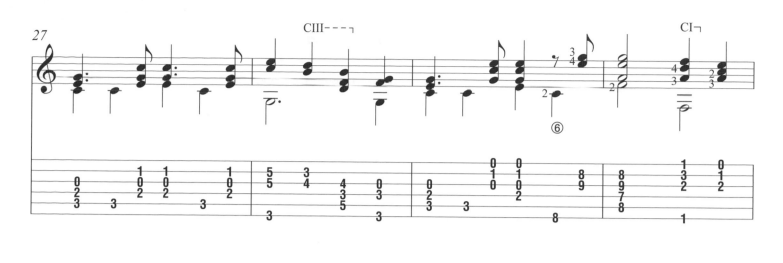

Coda

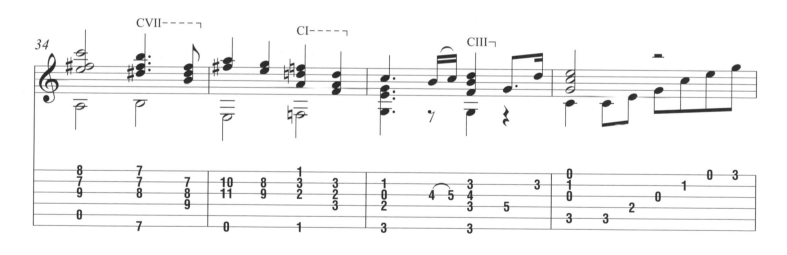

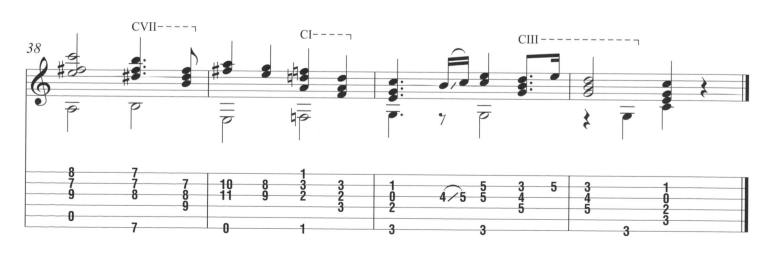

Dedicatoria

Enrique Granados
Arranged by Bridget Mermikides

Drop D tuning:
(low to high) D-A-D-G-B-E

Alla Hornpipe

George Frideric Handel
Arranged by Bridget Mermikides

Drop D tuning:
(low to high) D-A-D-G-B-E

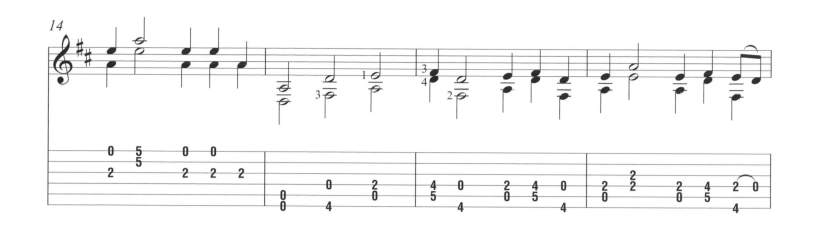

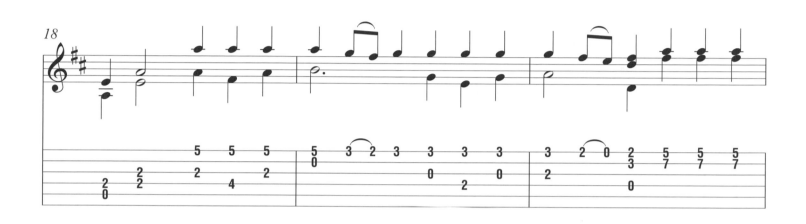

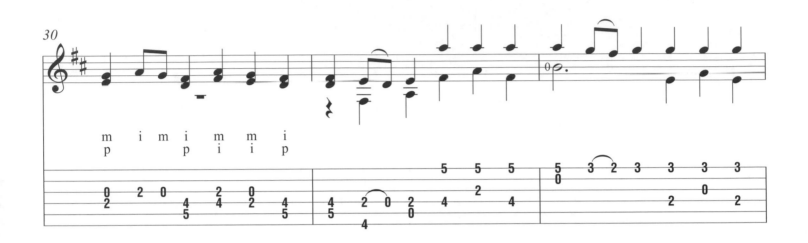

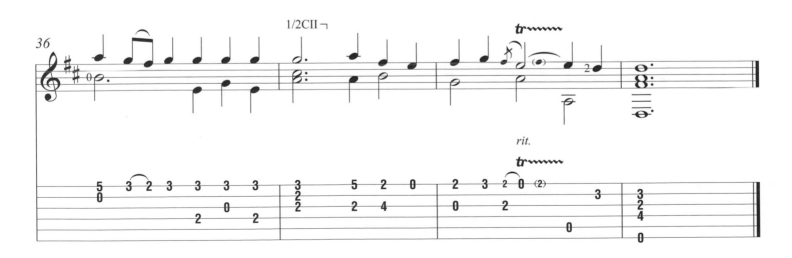

Aria from Rinaldo
(Lascia ch'io pianga)

George Frideric Handel
Arranged by Bridget Mermikides

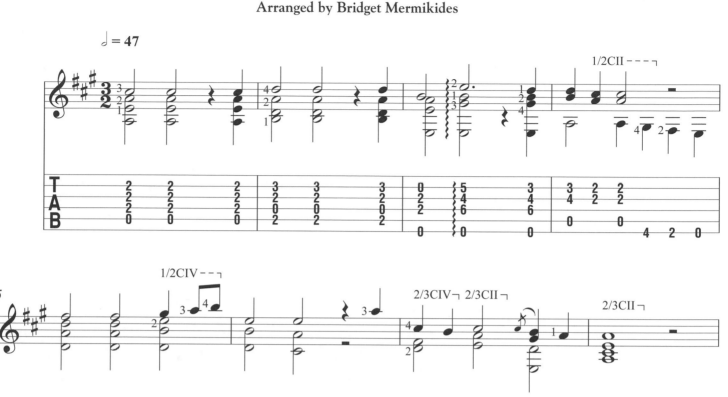

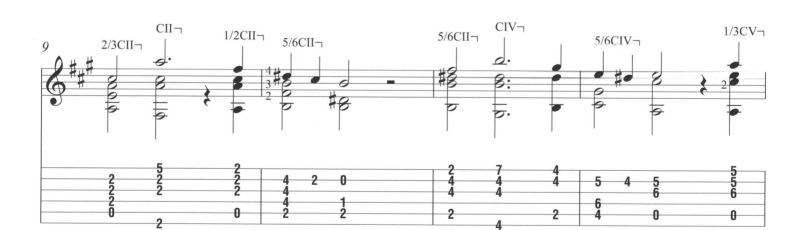

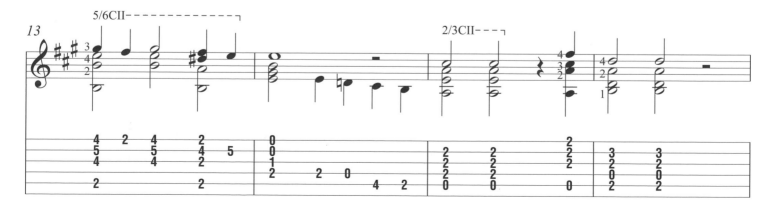

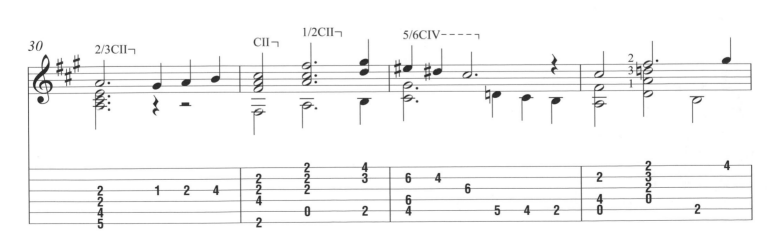

Ombra mai fu

George Frideric Handel
Arranged by Bridget Mermikides

Drop D tuning:
(low to high) D-A-D-G-B-E

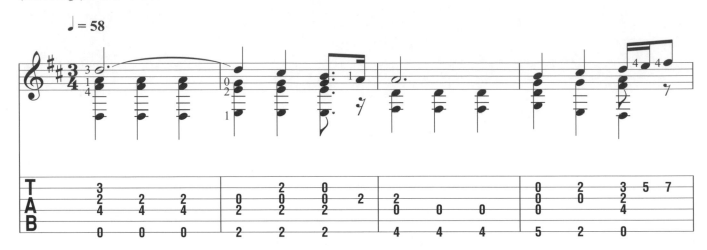

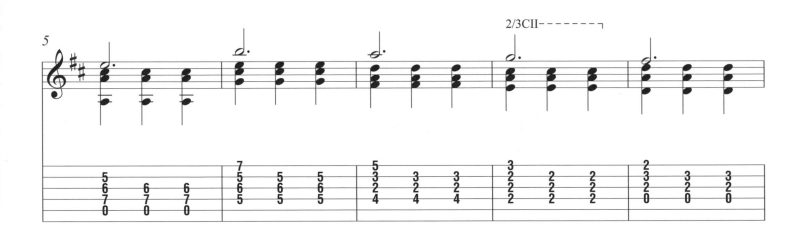

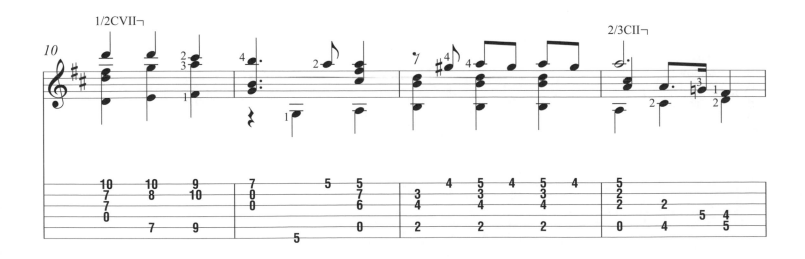

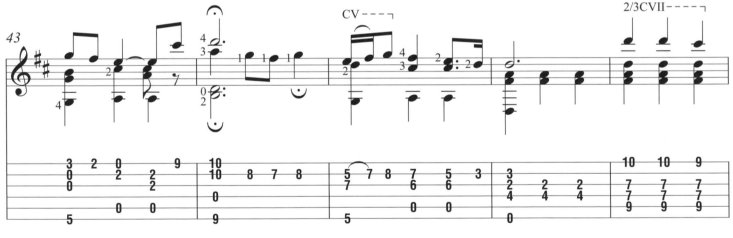

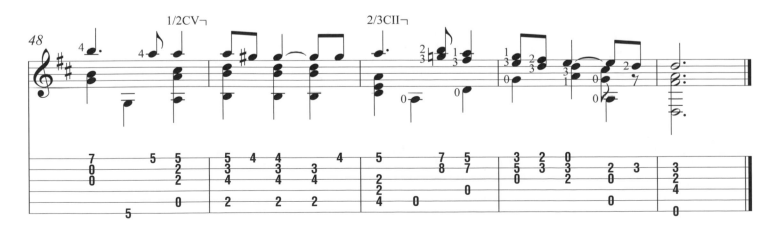

I Vow to Thee My Country

Gustav Holst
Arranged by Bridget Mermikides

Drop D tuning:
(low to high) D-A-D-G-B-E

♩ = 80

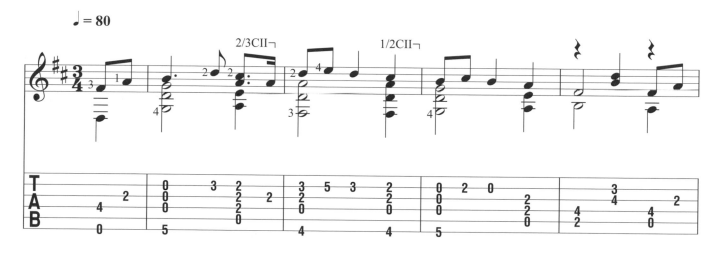

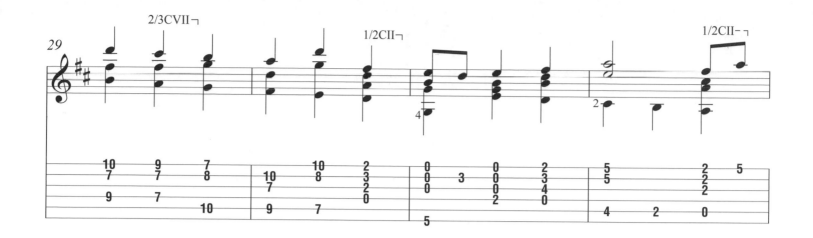

Alman

Robert Johnson
Edited by Bridget Mermikides

$\quad = 105$

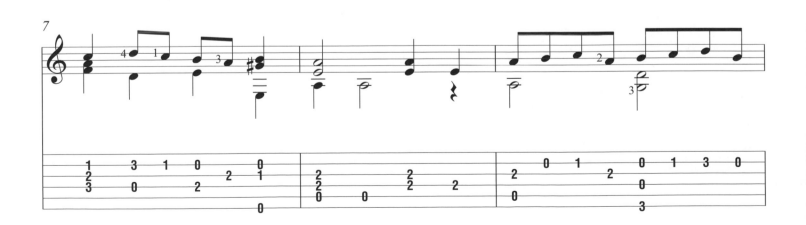

Adagio from Oboe Concerto

Alessandro Marcello

Arranged by Bridget Mermikides

Drop D tuning:
(low to high) D-A-D-G-B-E

♩ = 30

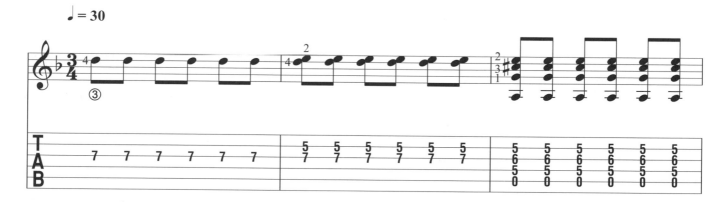

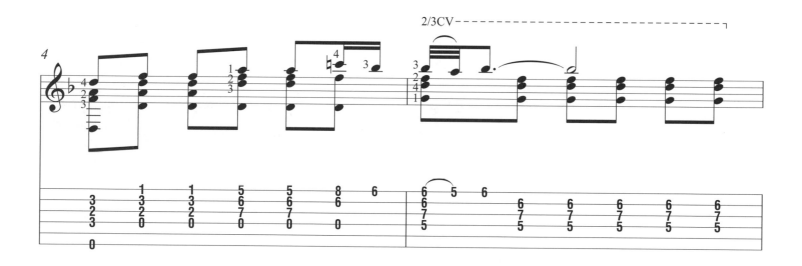

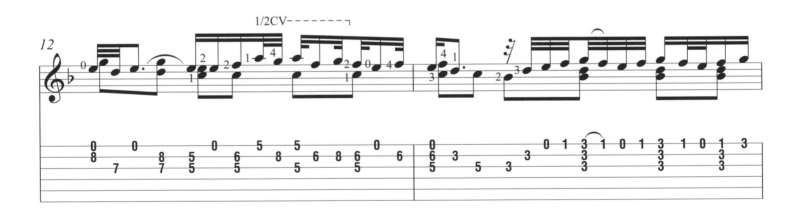

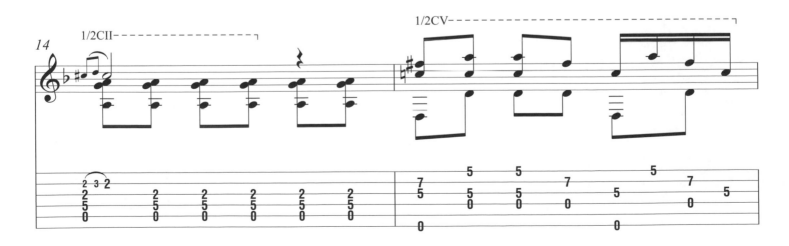

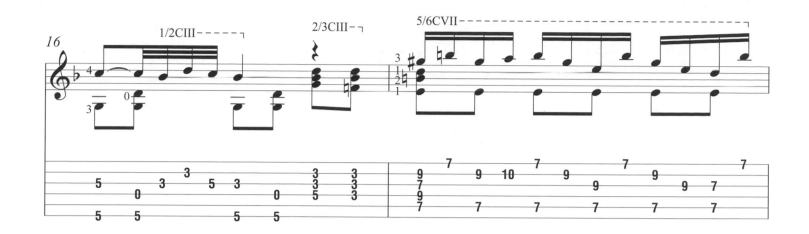

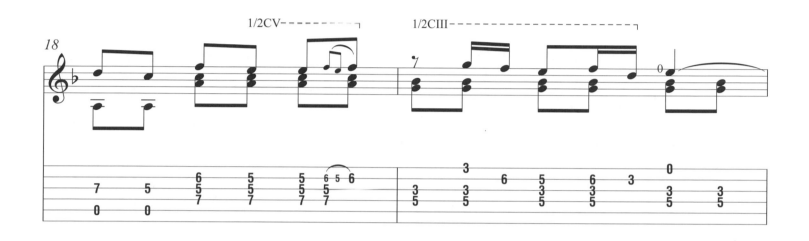

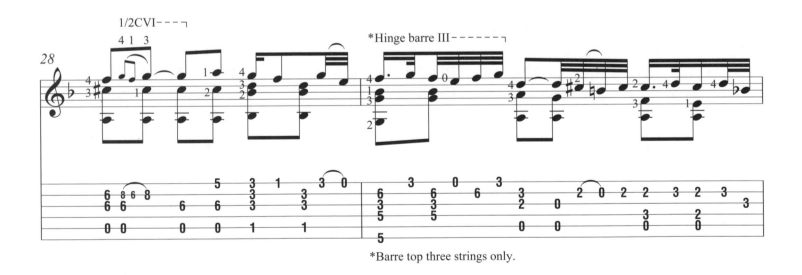

*Barre top three strings only.

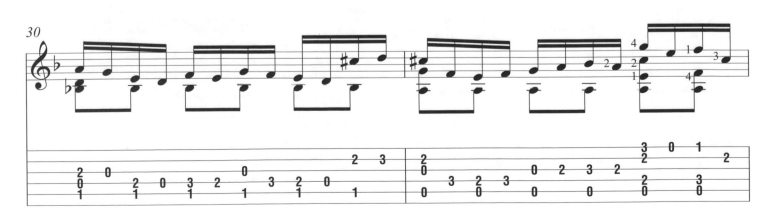

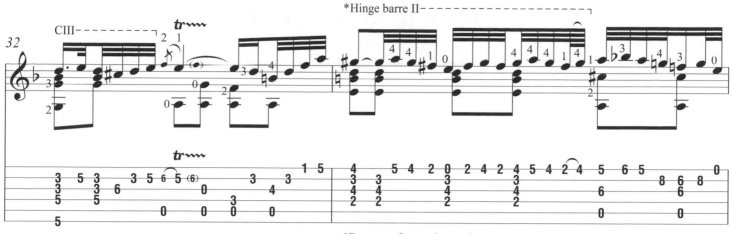

*Hinge barre II-- - - - - - - - - - - - - - - -

CIII- - - - - - - - - -

*Barre top four strings only.

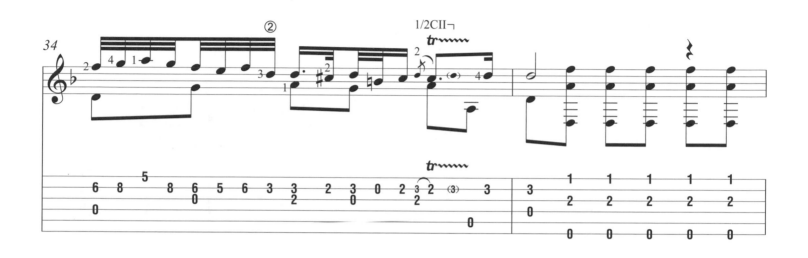

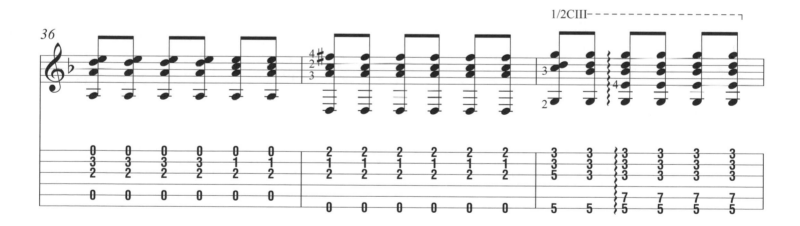

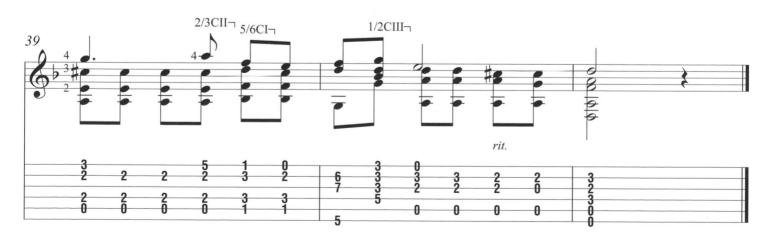

rit.

Abide with Me

William Henry Monk
Arranged by Bridget Mermikides

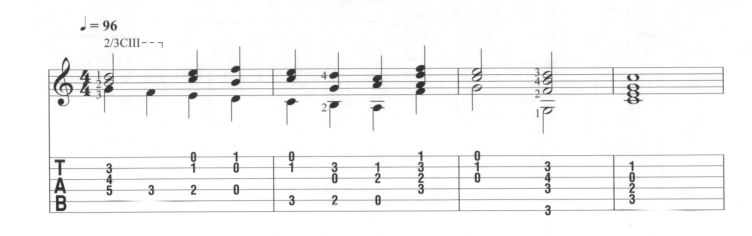

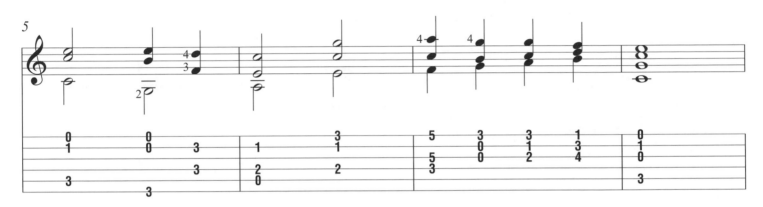

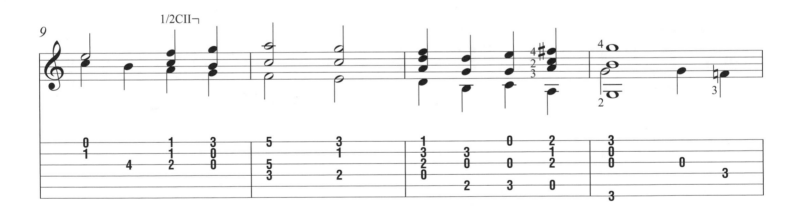

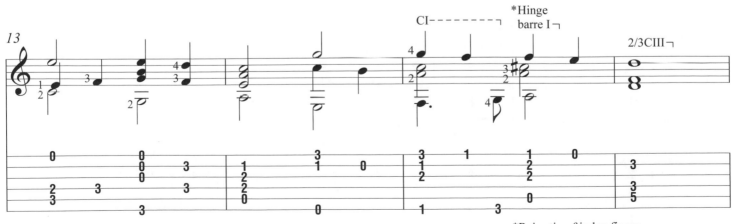

*Raise tip of index finger.

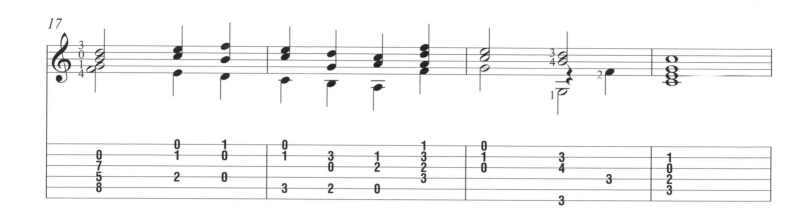

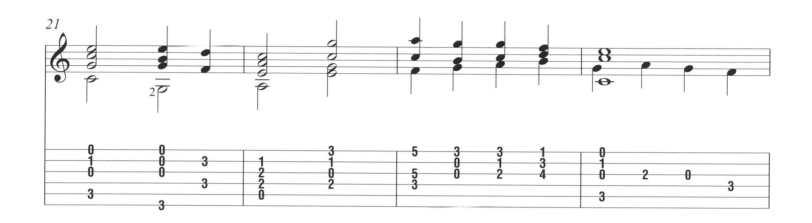

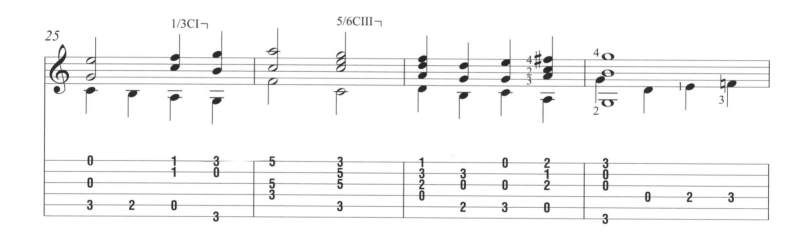

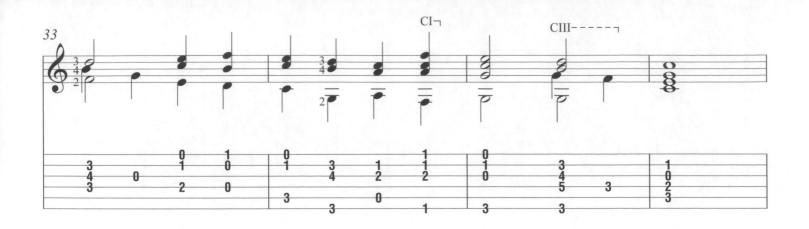

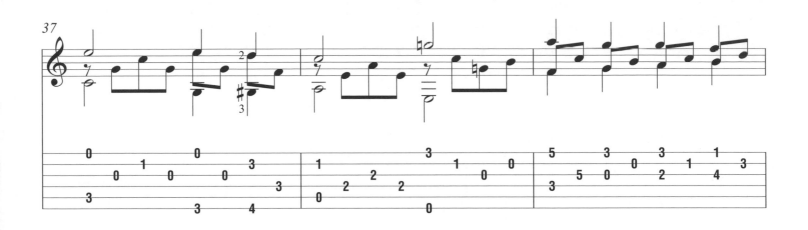

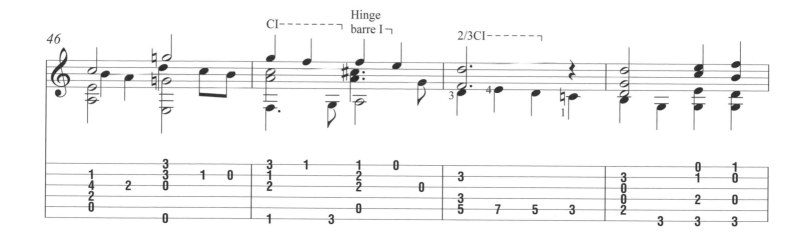

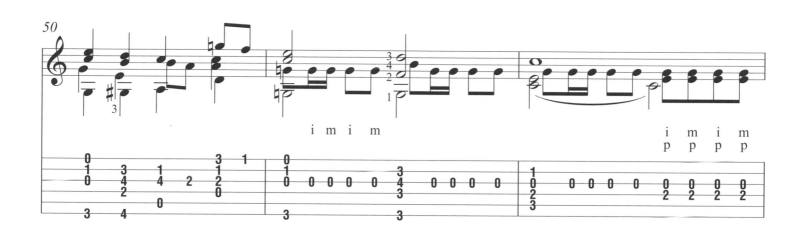

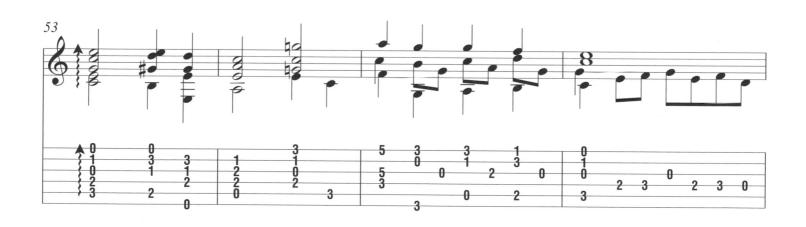

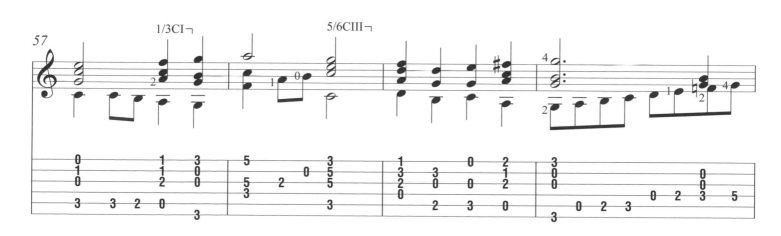

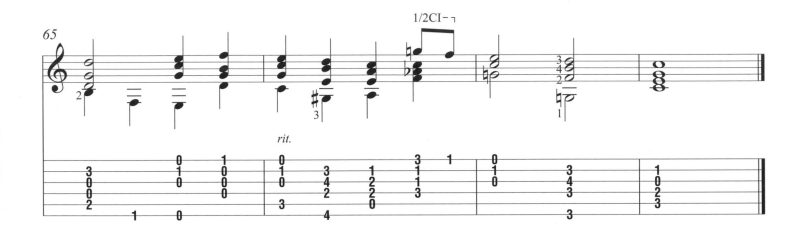

78

Ave verum corpus

Wolfgang Amadeus Mozart
Arranged by Bridget Mermikides

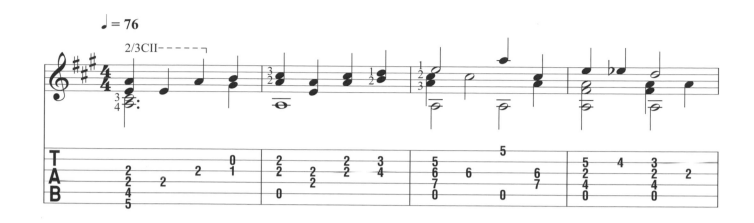

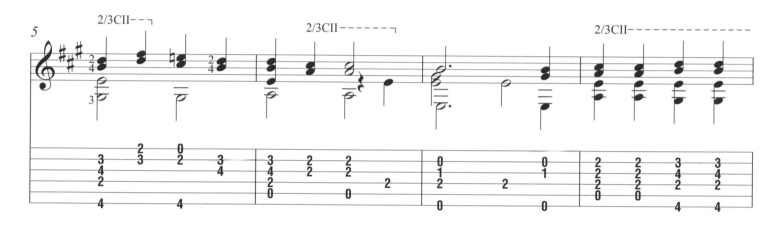

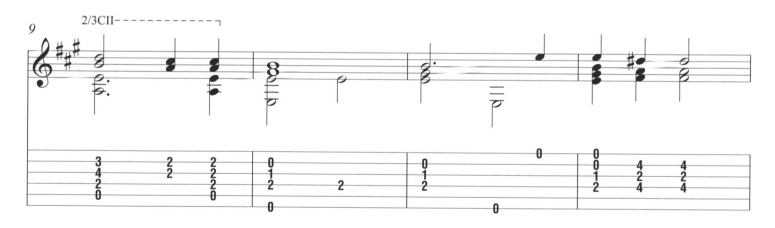

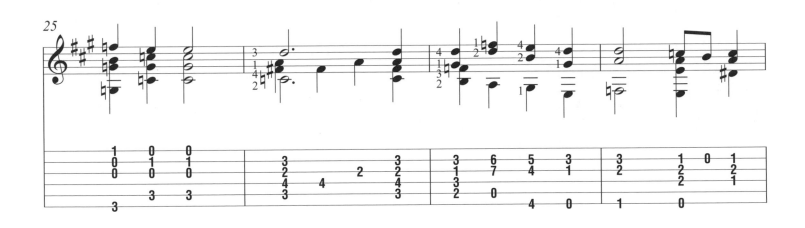

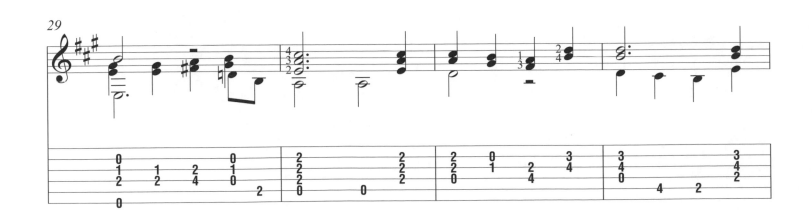

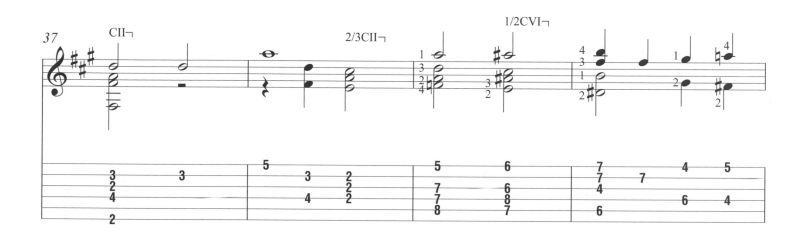

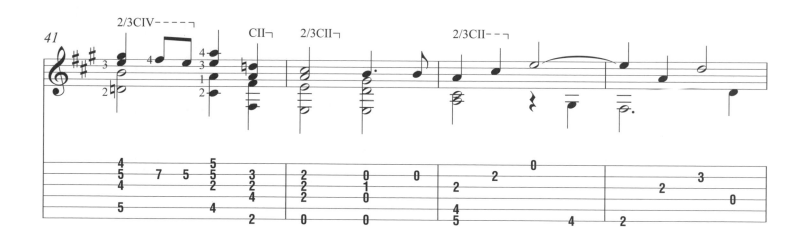

Duet "Sull'aria... Che soave zeffiretto"
from The Marriage of Figaro

Wolfgang Amadeus Mozart
Arranged by Bridget Mermikides

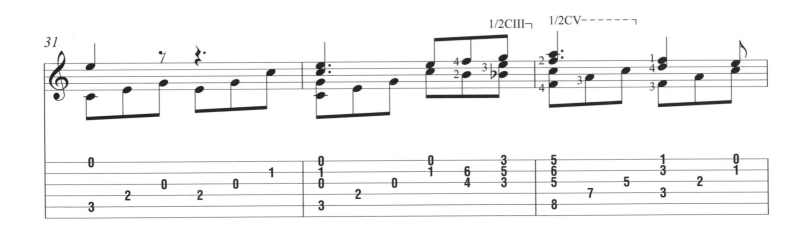

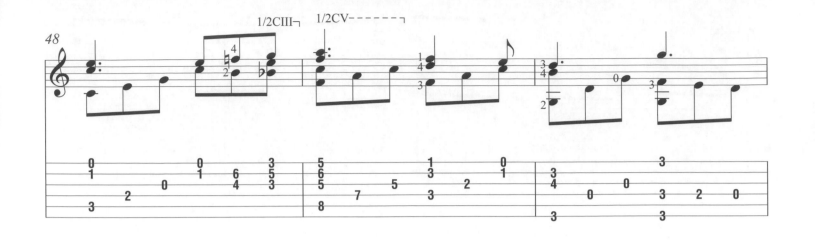

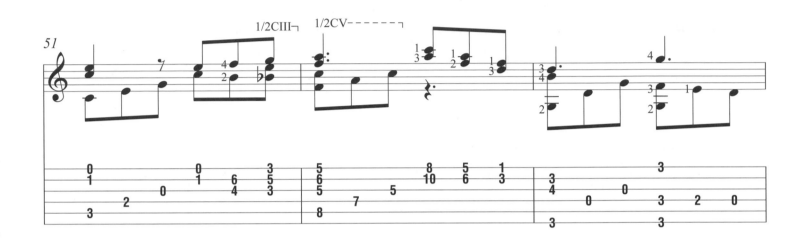

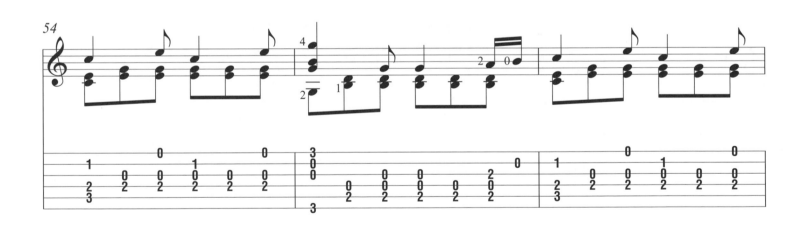

Fantasia no. 10

Alonso Mudarra
Edited by Bridget Mermikides

Tuning:

(low to high) E-A-D-F#-B-E

(Capo II optional)

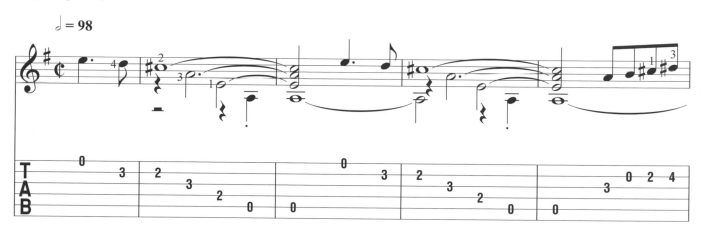

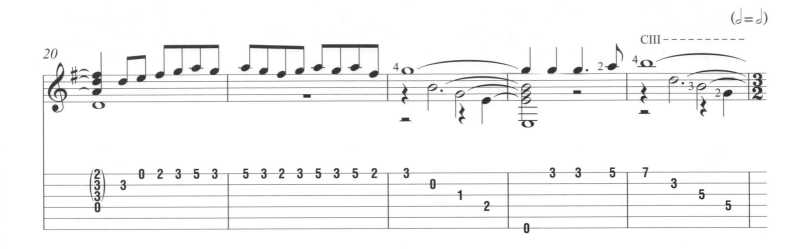

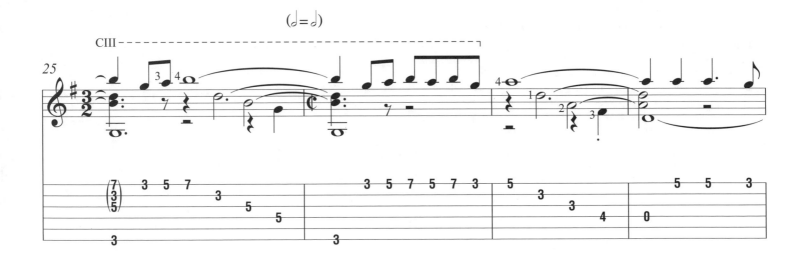

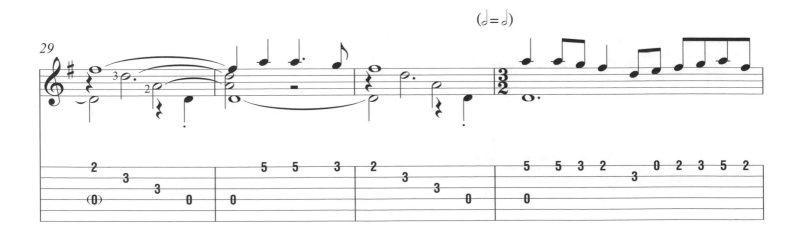

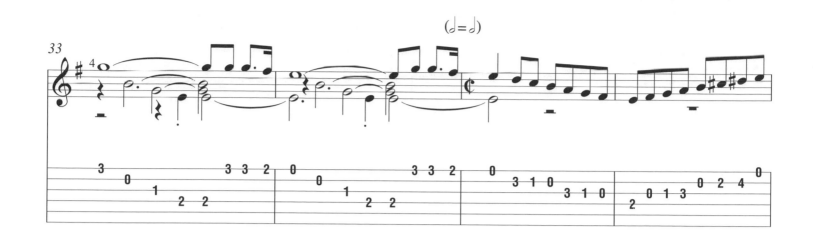

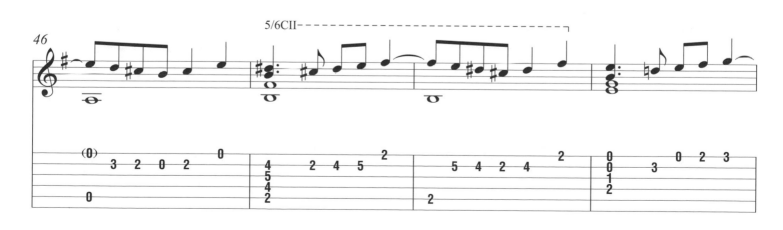

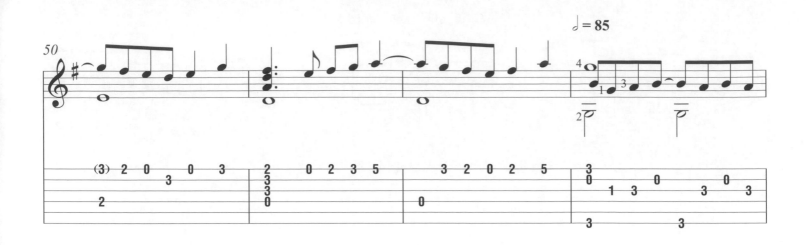

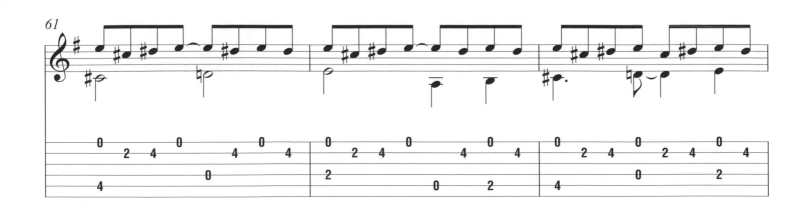

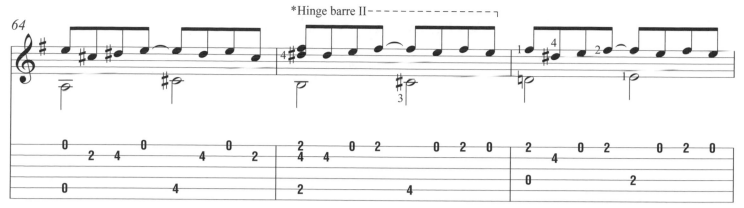

*Hinge barre II- - - - - - - - - - - - - - - - - - -

64

*Barre top five strings only.

67

70

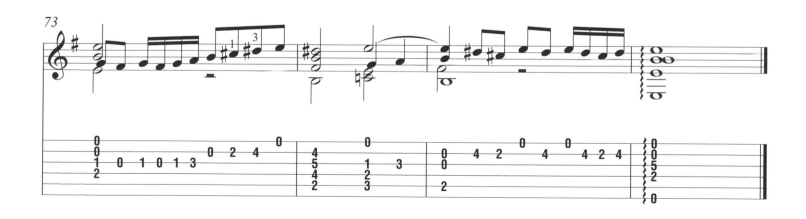

73

Amazing Grace

John Newton
Arranged by Bridget Mermikides

Drop D tuning:
(low to high) D-A-D-G-B-E

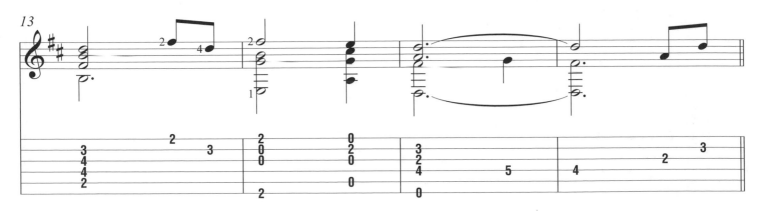

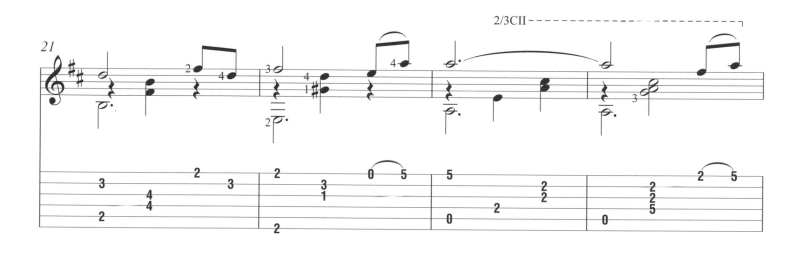

2/3CII -

*Hinge barre IV - - - ⌐

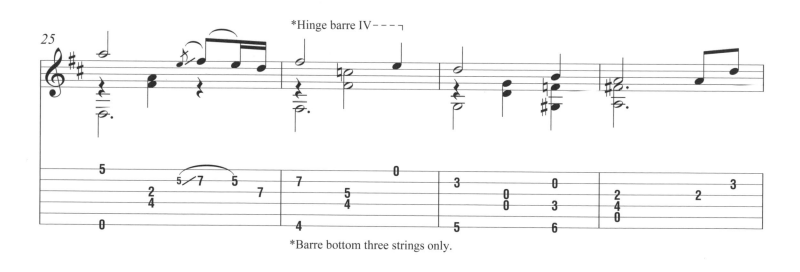

*Barre bottom three strings only.

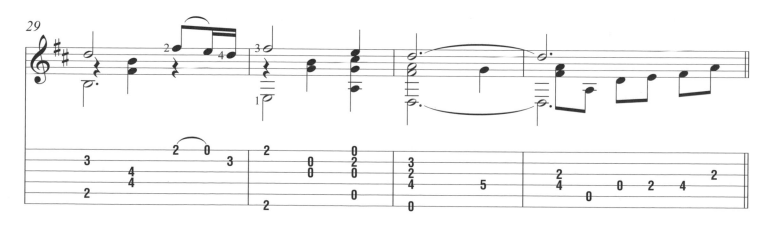

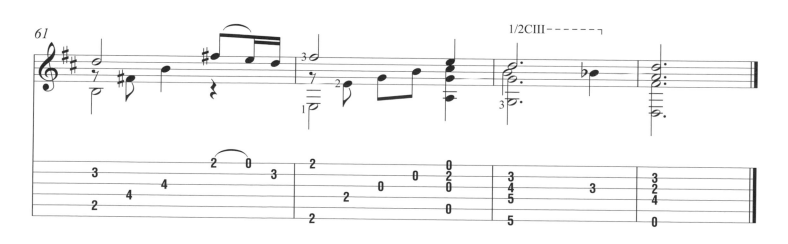

Un bel di vedremo

Giacomo Puccini
Arranged by Bridget Mermikides

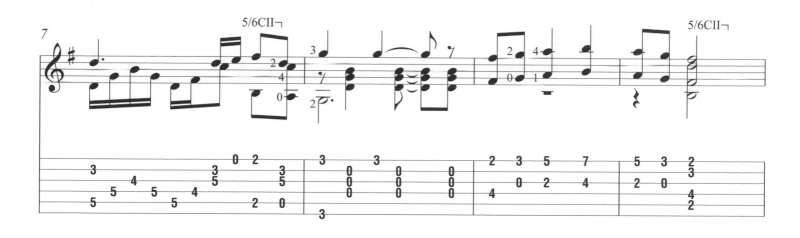

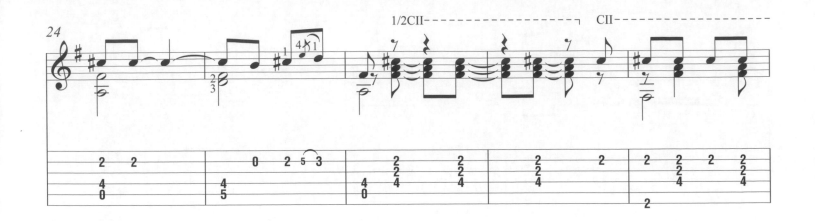

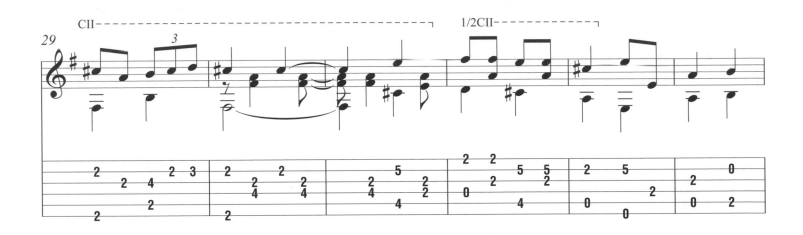

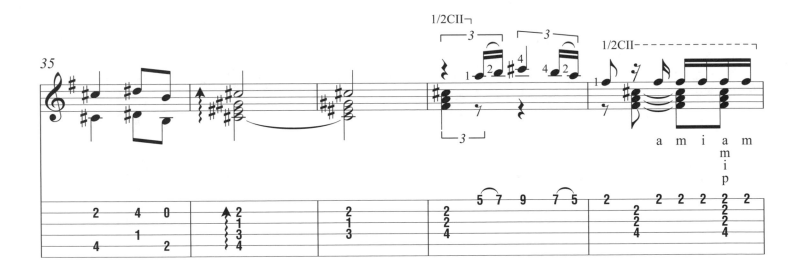

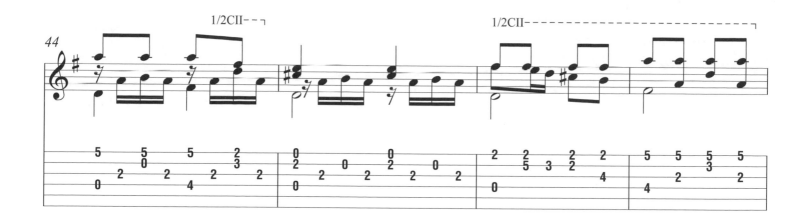

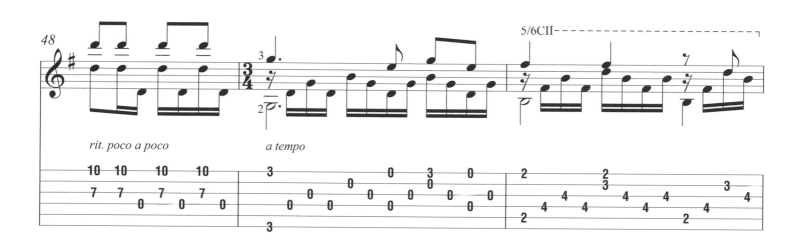

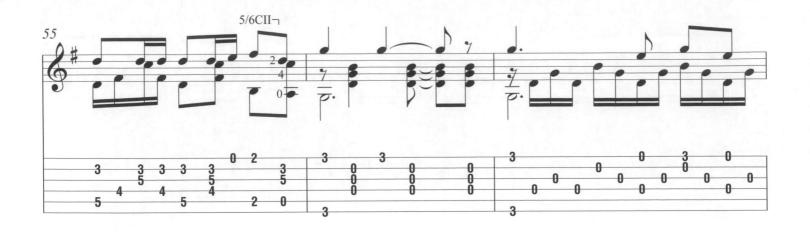

Rhapsody on a Theme of Paganini

Sergei Rachmaninov

Arranged by Bridget Mermikides

Drop D tuning:
(low to high) D-A-D-G-B-E

Andante cantabile ♩ = 46

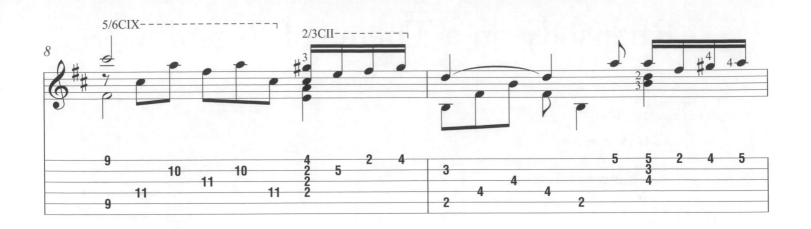

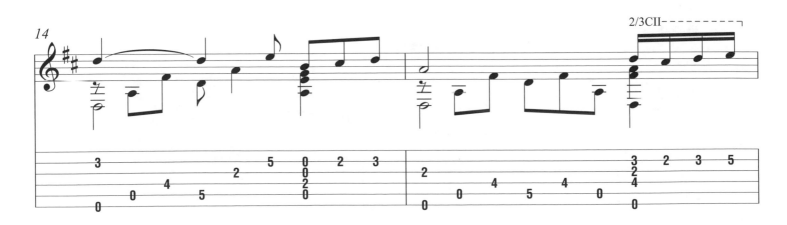

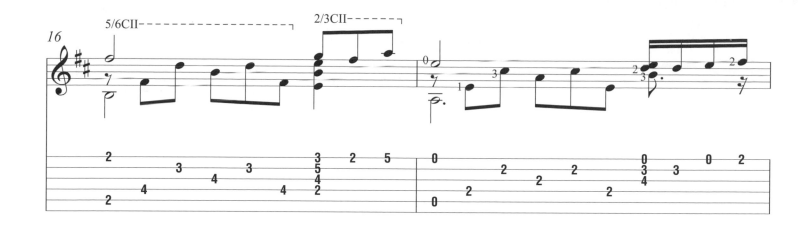

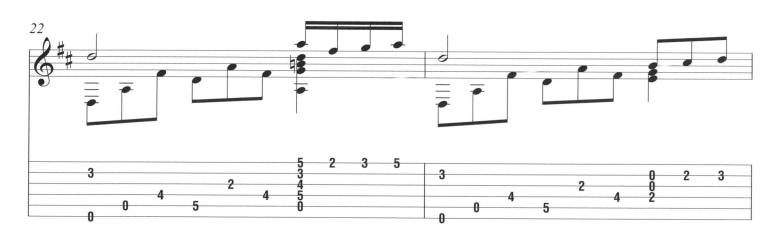

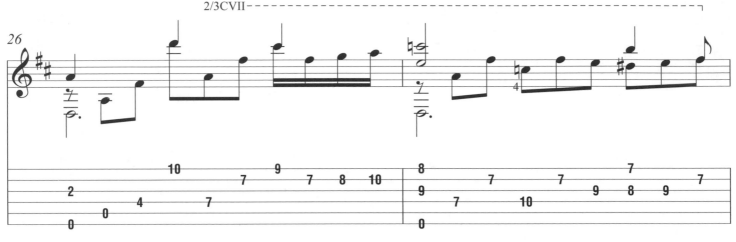

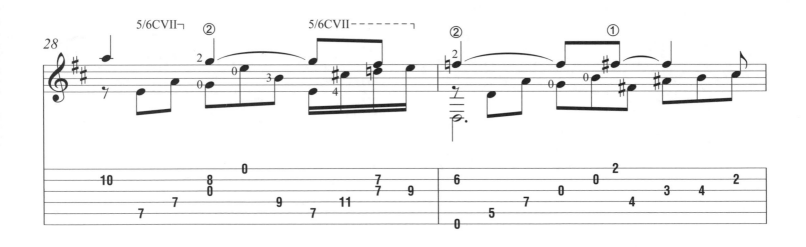

Vocalise

Sergei Rachmaninov
Arranged by Bridget Mermikides

*Slant barre (tip of index finger still on low F#)

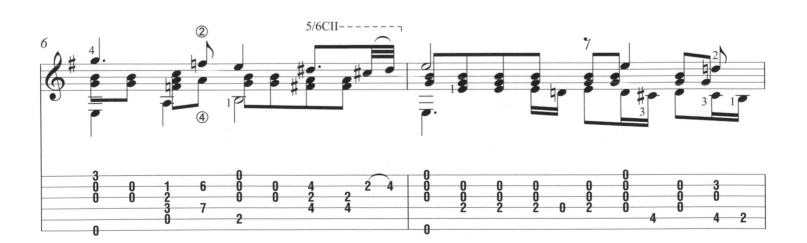

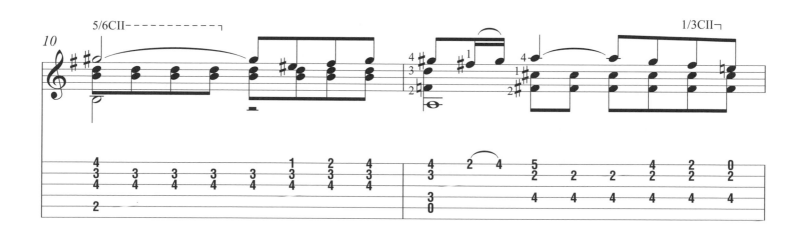

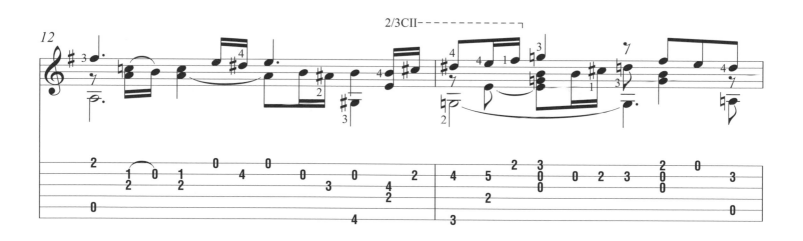

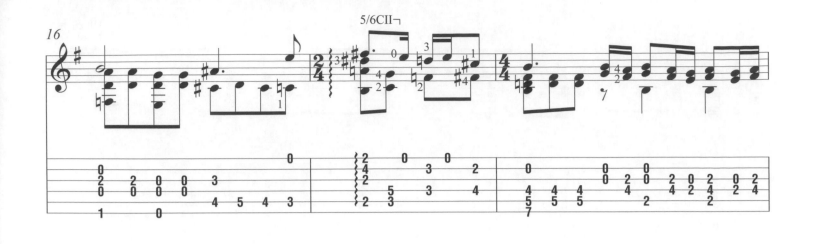

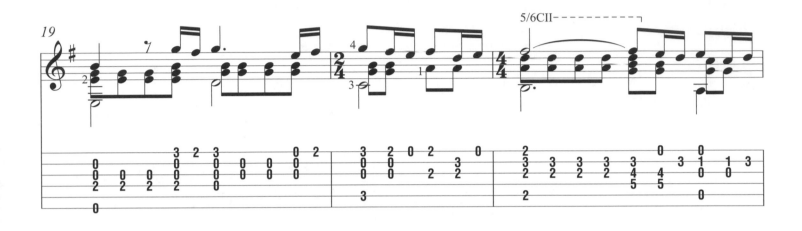

*Slant barre

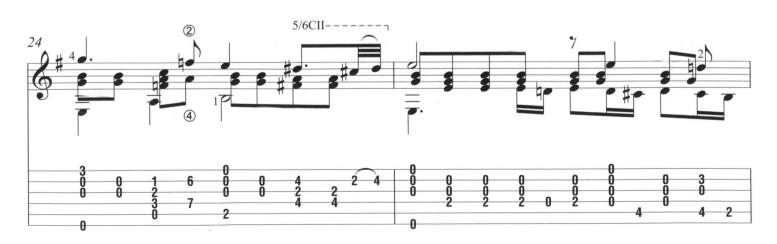

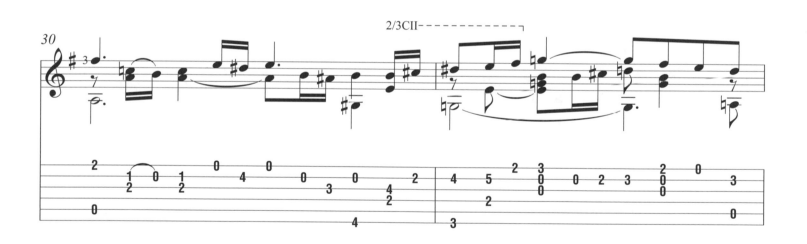

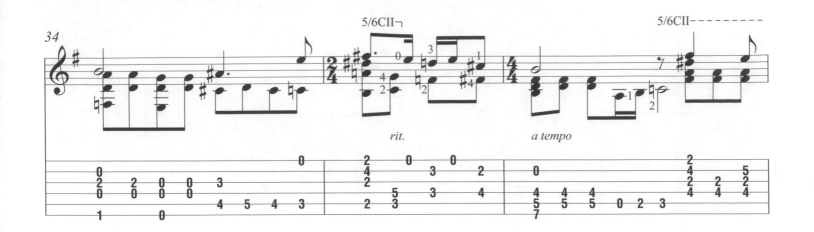

*Raise tip of index finger.

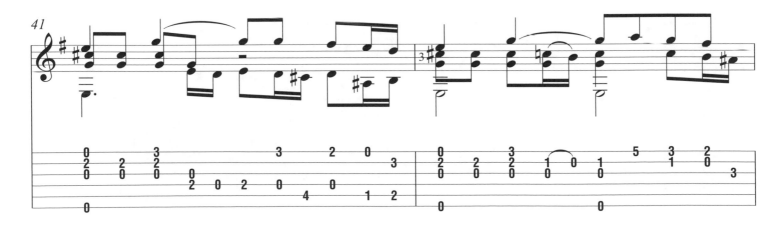

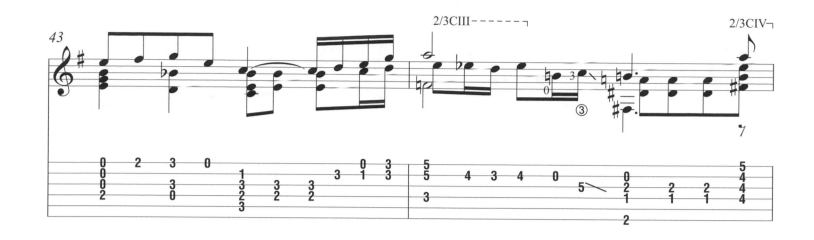

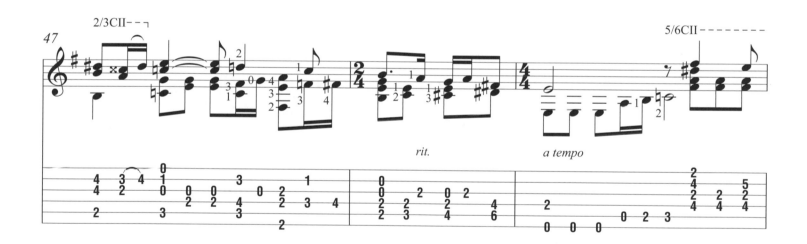

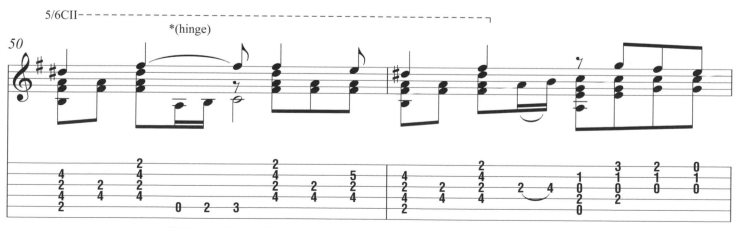

*Raise tip of index finger.

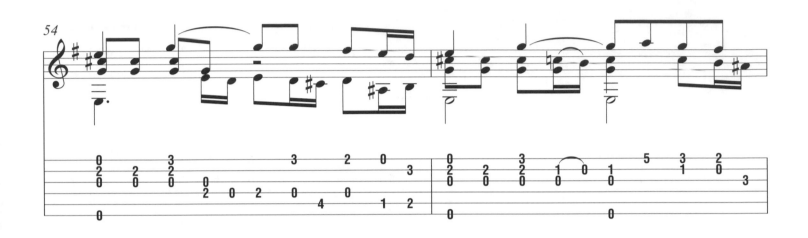

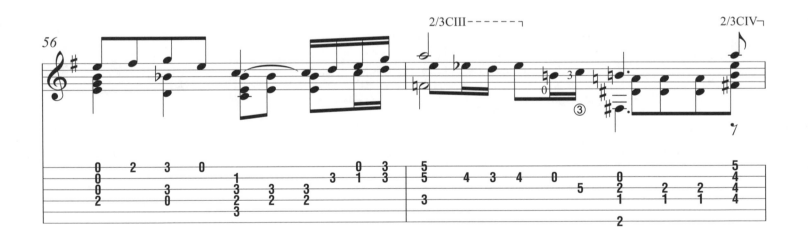

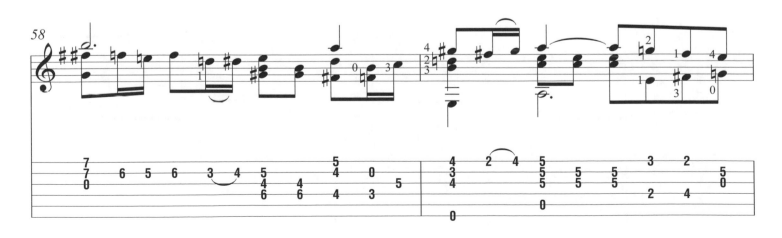

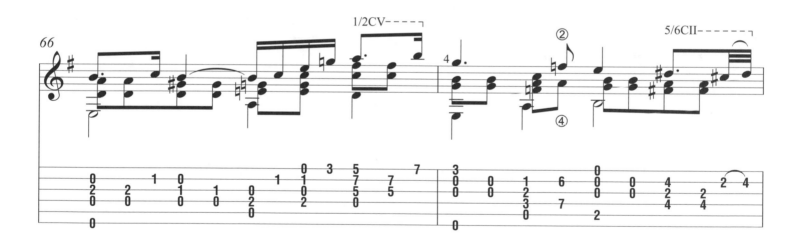

*Slant barre

Canarios

Gaspar Sanz
Edited by Bridget Mermikides

Drop D tuning:
(low to high) D-A-D-G-B-E

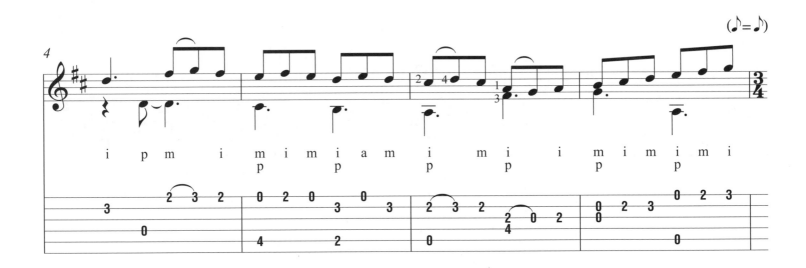

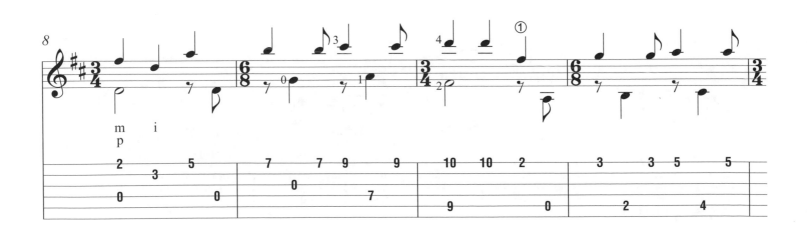

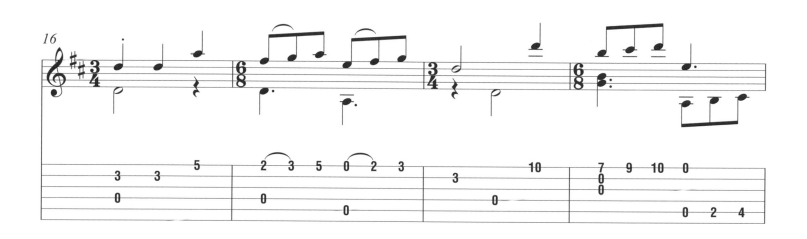

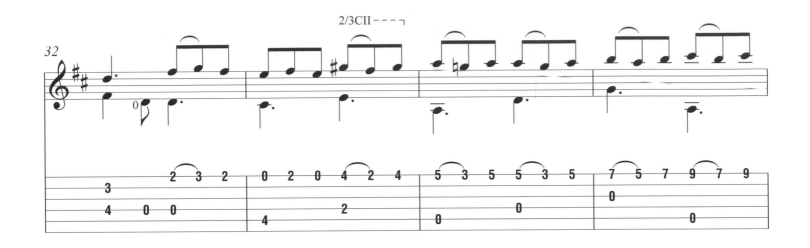

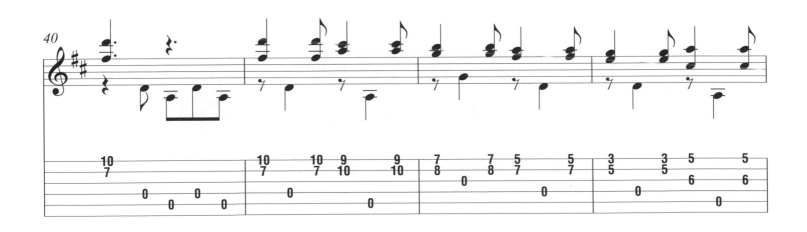

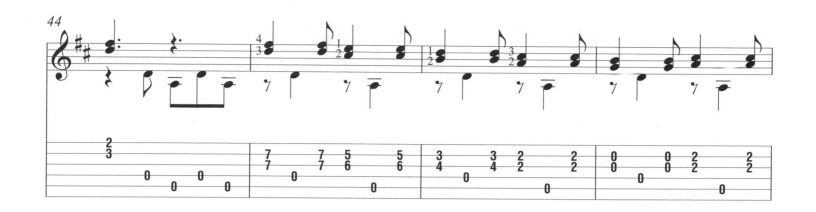

Serenade - Swan Song no. 4

Franz Schubert
Arranged by Bridget Mermikides

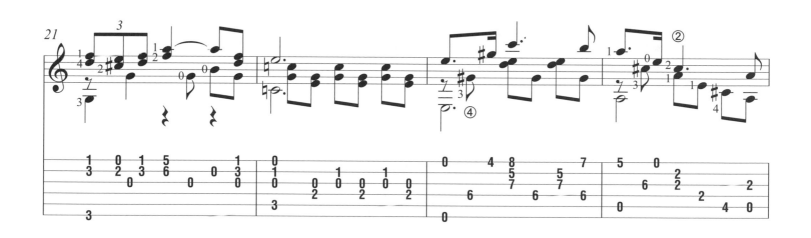

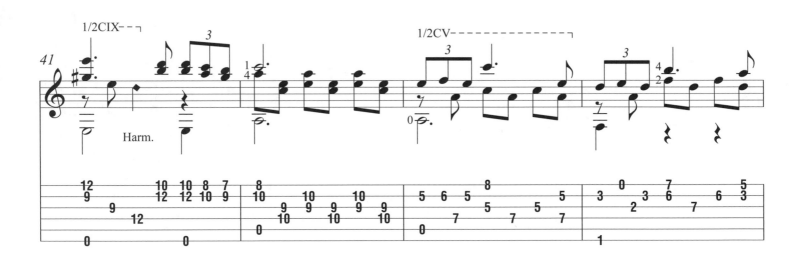

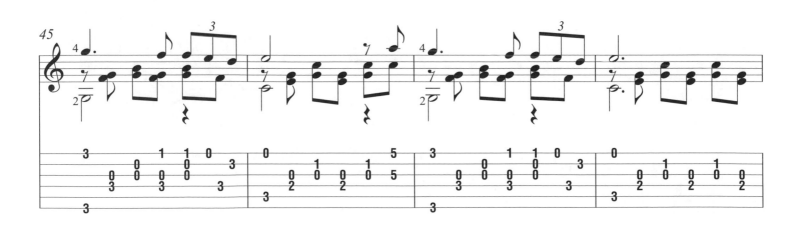

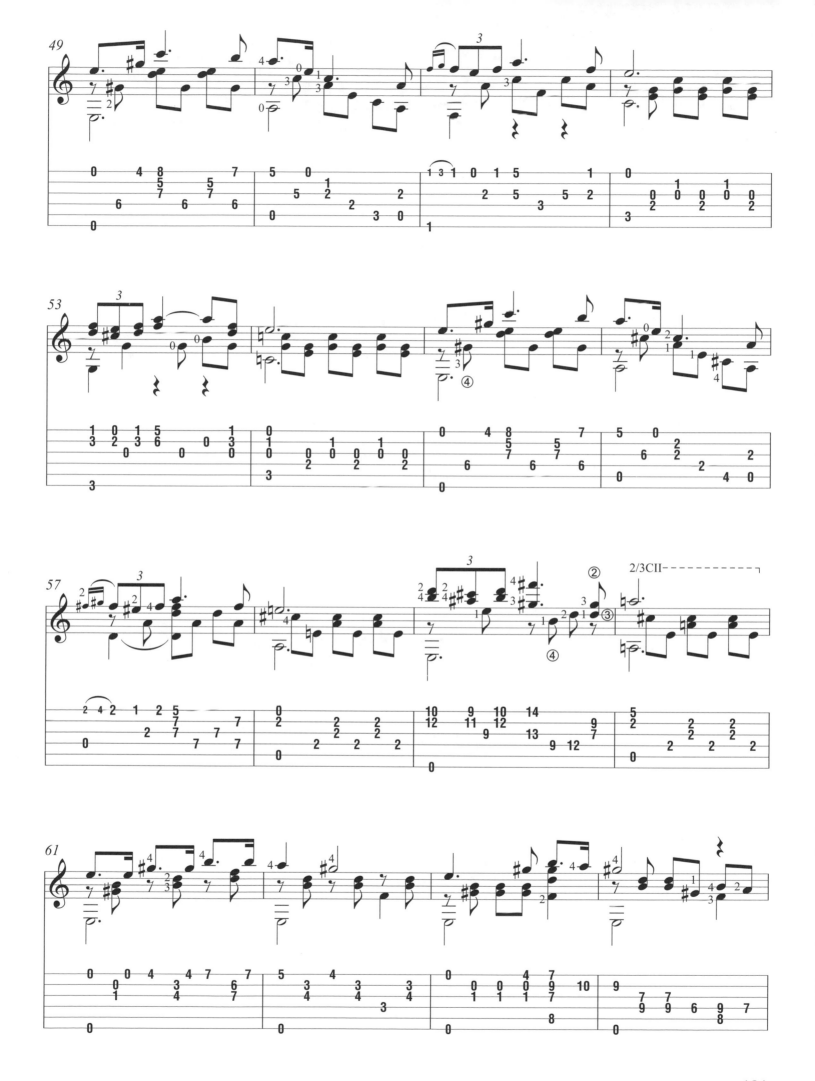

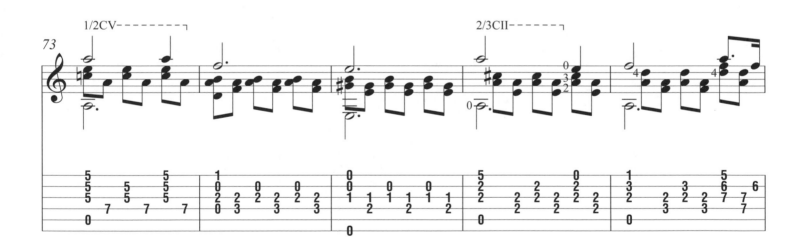

122

Of Foreign Lands and People

Robert Schumann
Arranged by Bridget Mermikides

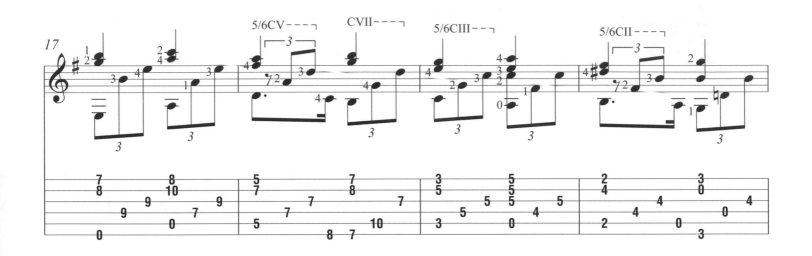

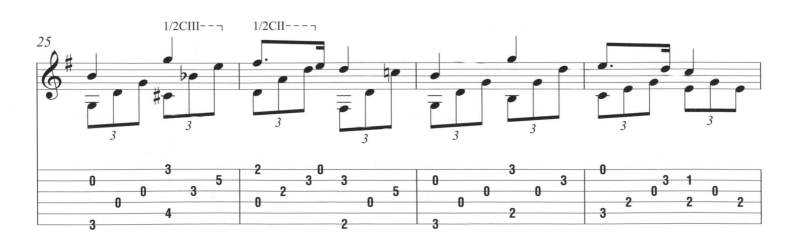

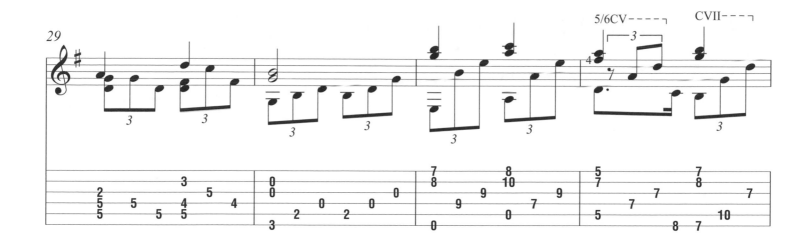

The Liberty Bell March

John Philip Sousa
Arranged by Bridget Mermikides

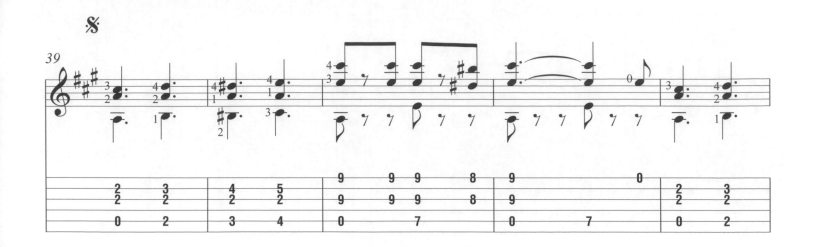

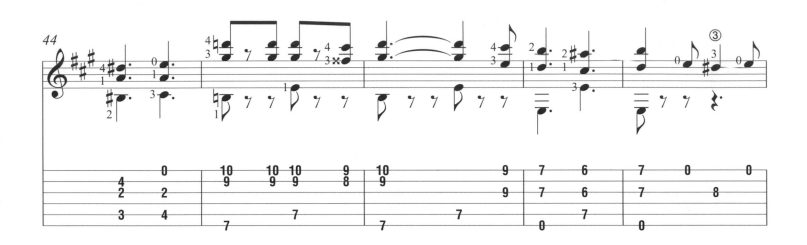

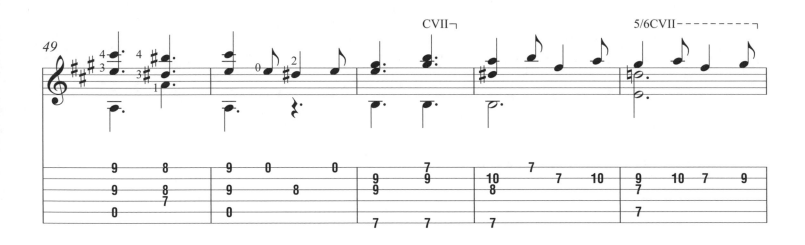

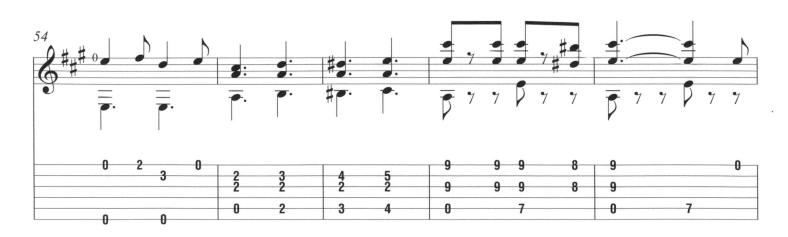

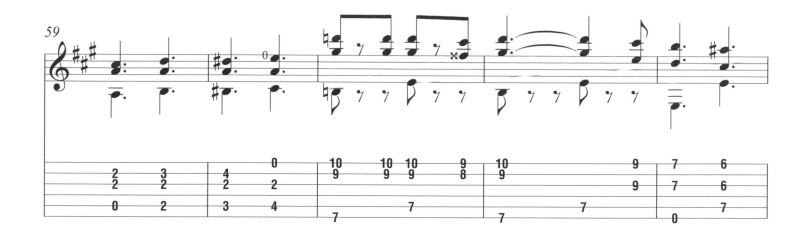

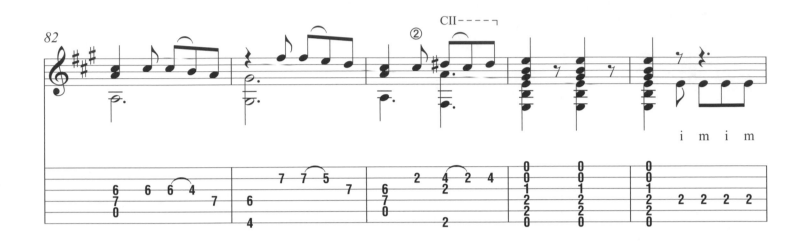

♭ Coda

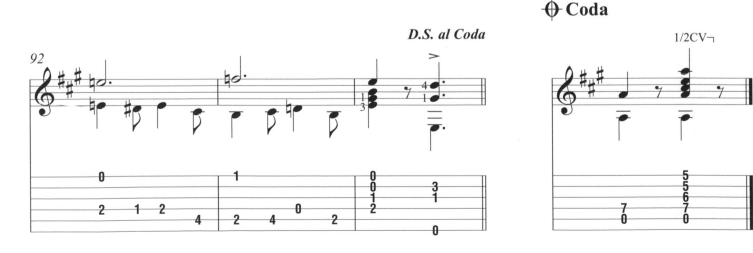

Capricho Arabe

Francisco Tarrega
Edited by Bridget Mermikides

Drop D tuning:
(low to high) D-A-D-G-B-E

Andantino

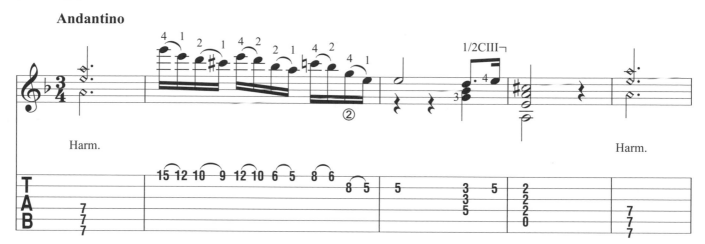

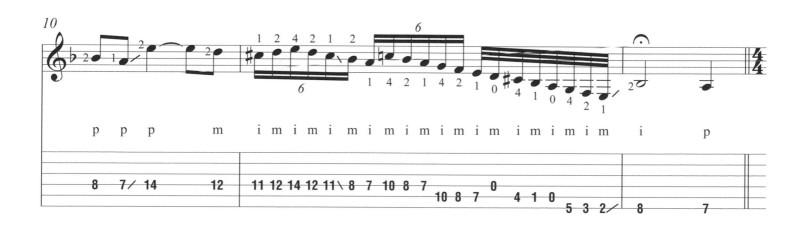

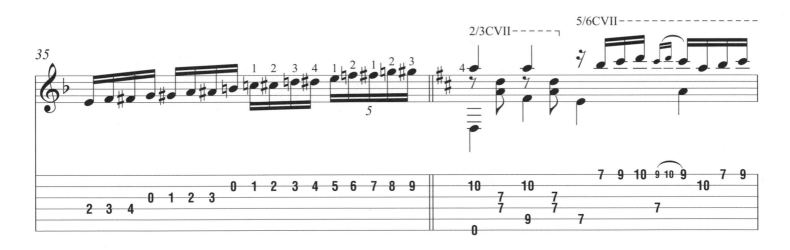

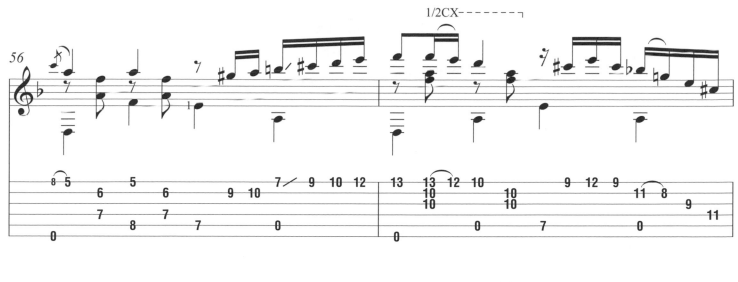

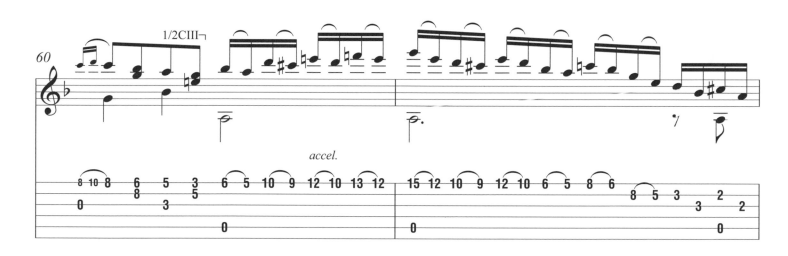

Pavana

Francisco Tarrega
Edited by Bridget Mermikides

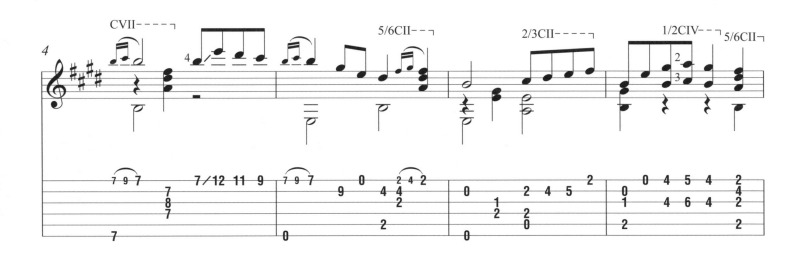

Dance of the Little Swans

Pyotr Ilyich Tchaikovsky
Arranged by Bridget Mermikides

Drop D tuning:
(low to high) D-A-D-G-B-E

♩ = 81

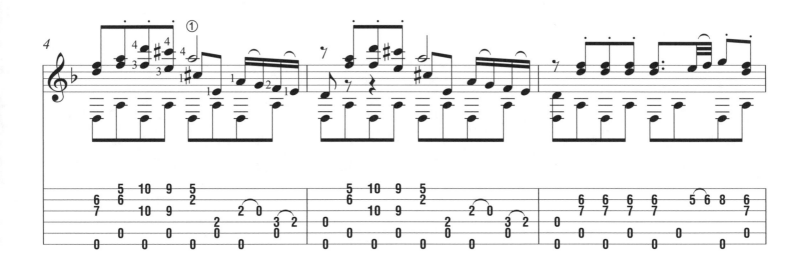

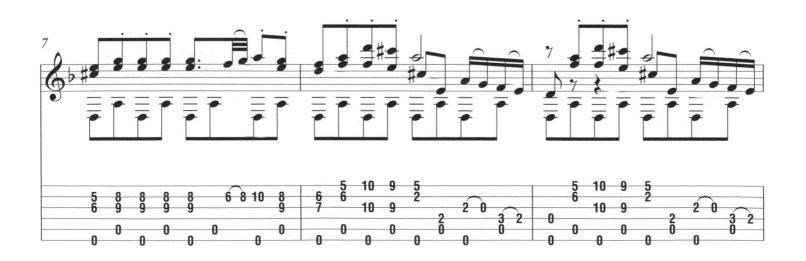

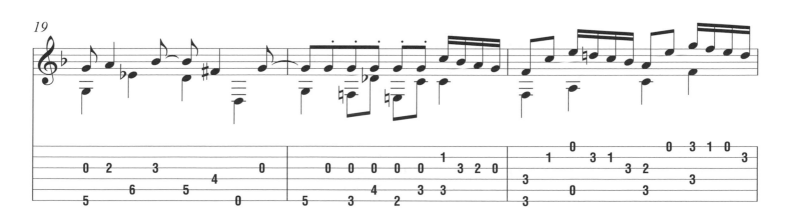

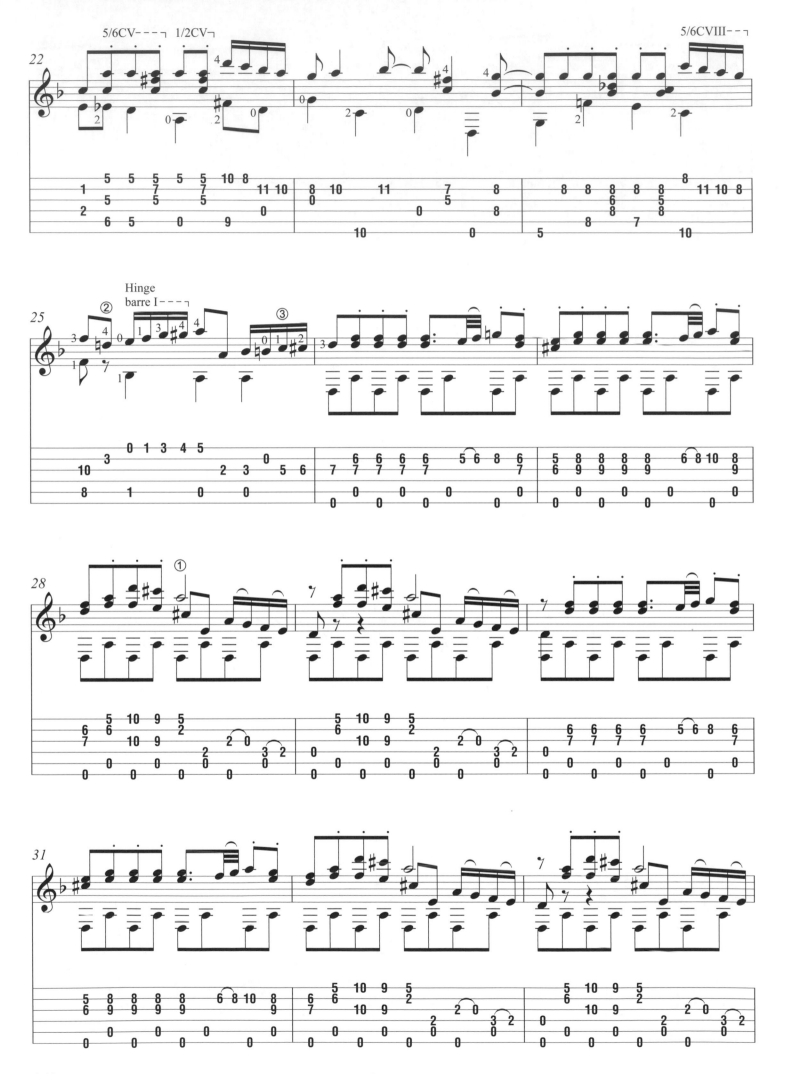

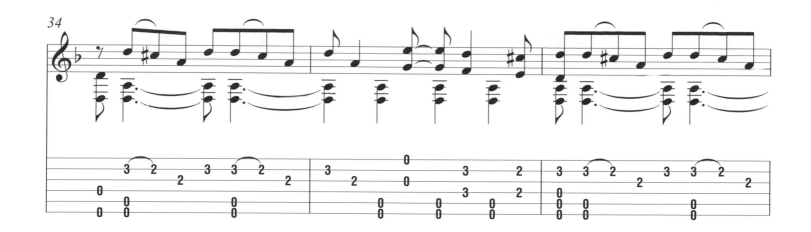

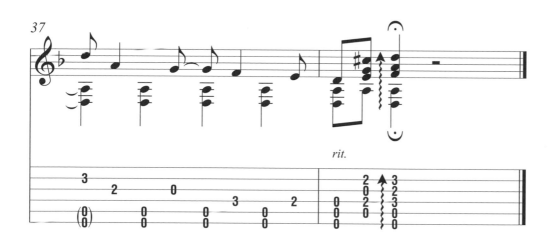

Dance of the Reed Pipes

Pyotr Ilyich Tchaikovsky
Arranged by Bridget Mermikides

Drop D tuning:
(low to high) D-A-D-G-B-E

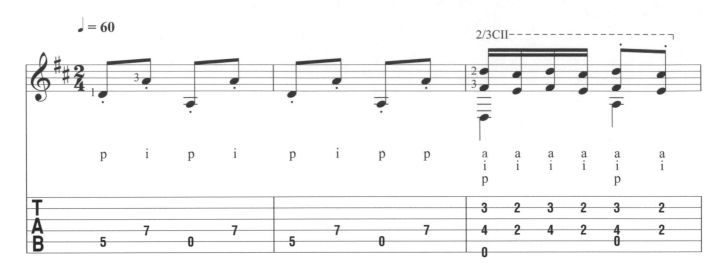

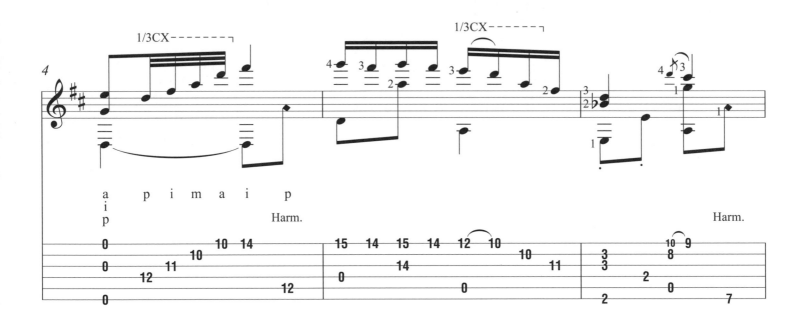

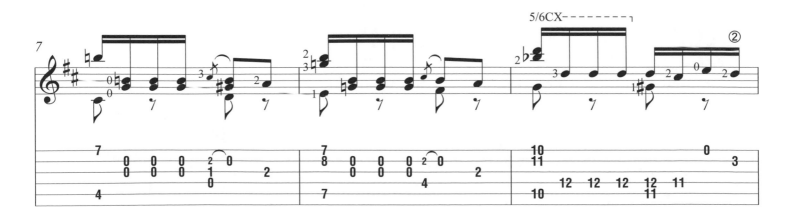

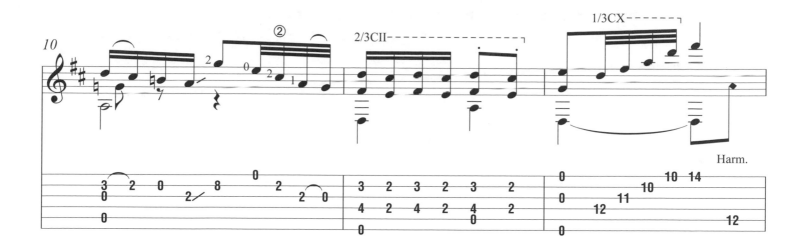

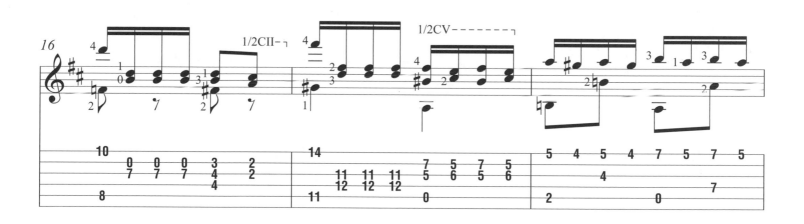

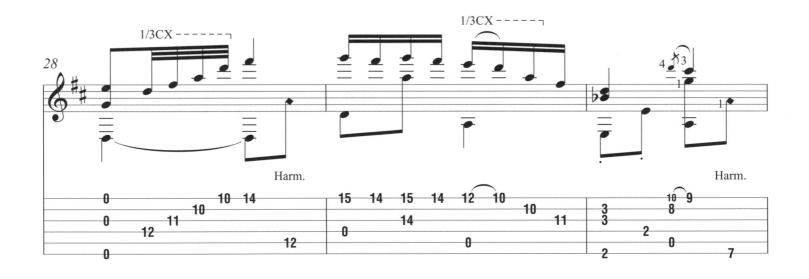

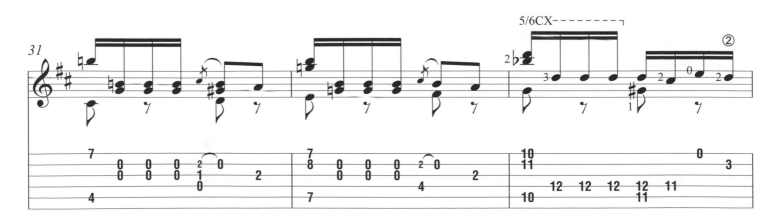

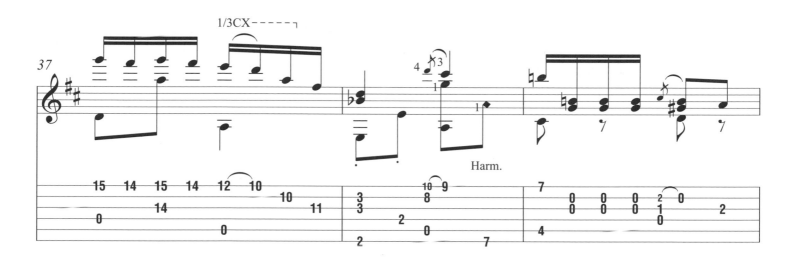

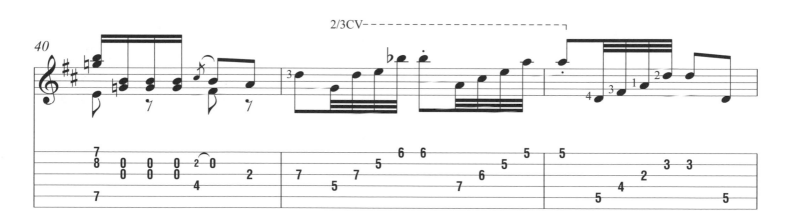

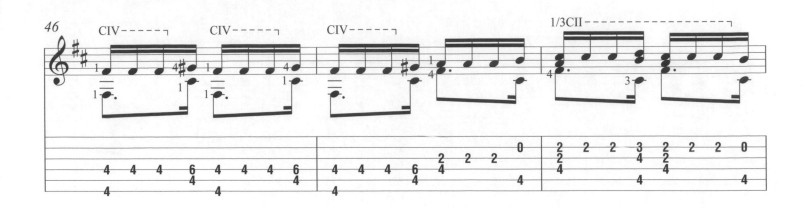

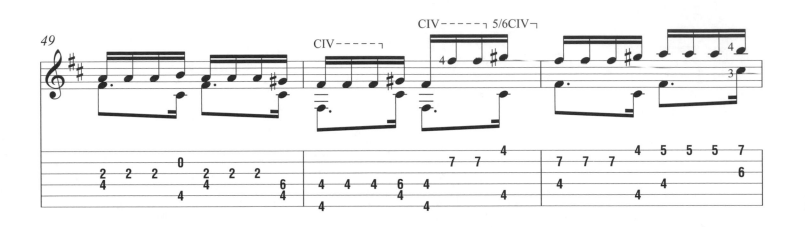

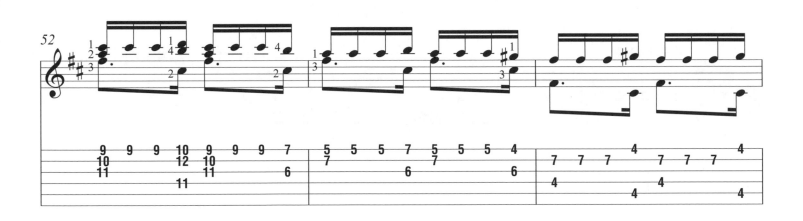

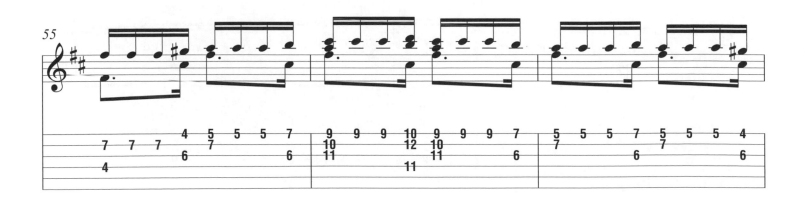

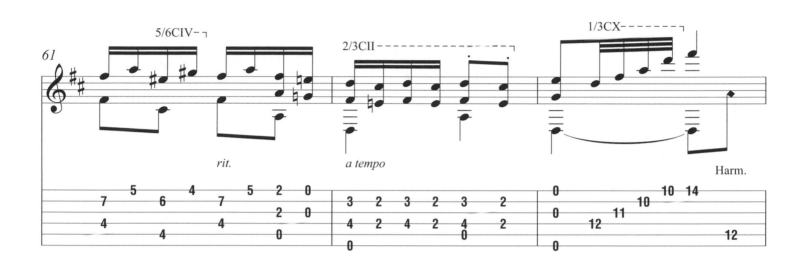

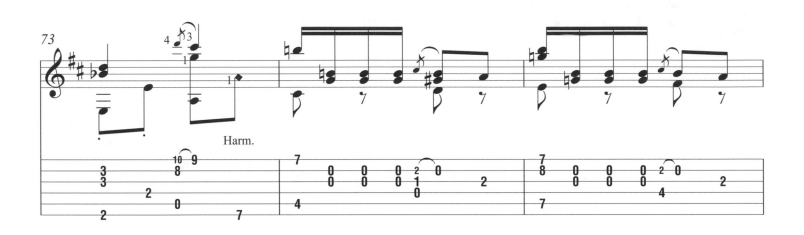

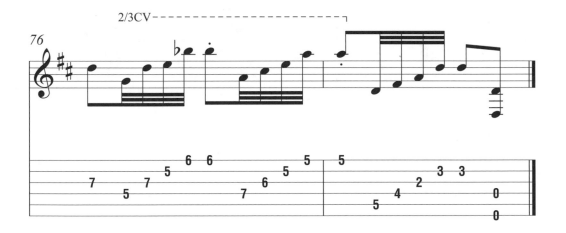

Hearts and Flowers

Theodore Moses Tobani
Arranged by Bridget Mermikides

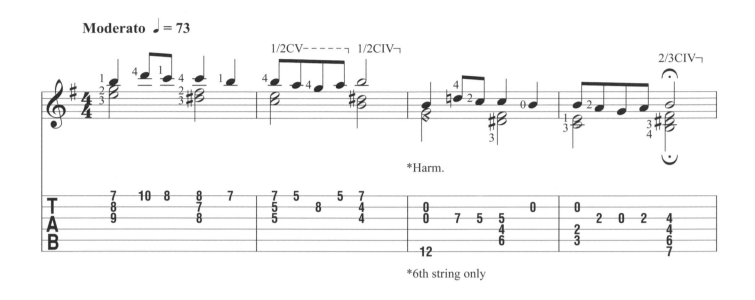

*Harm.

*6th string only

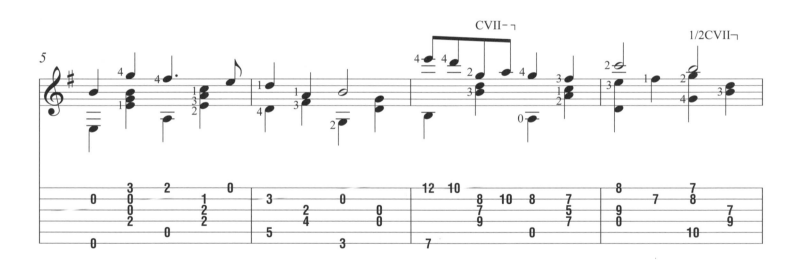

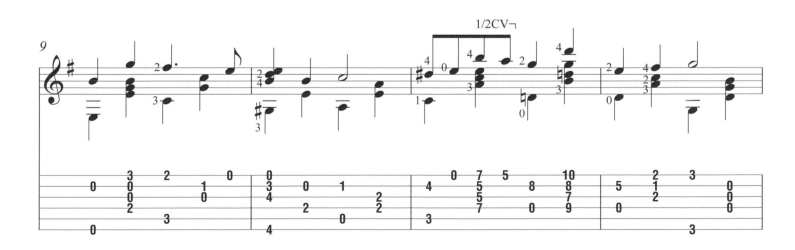

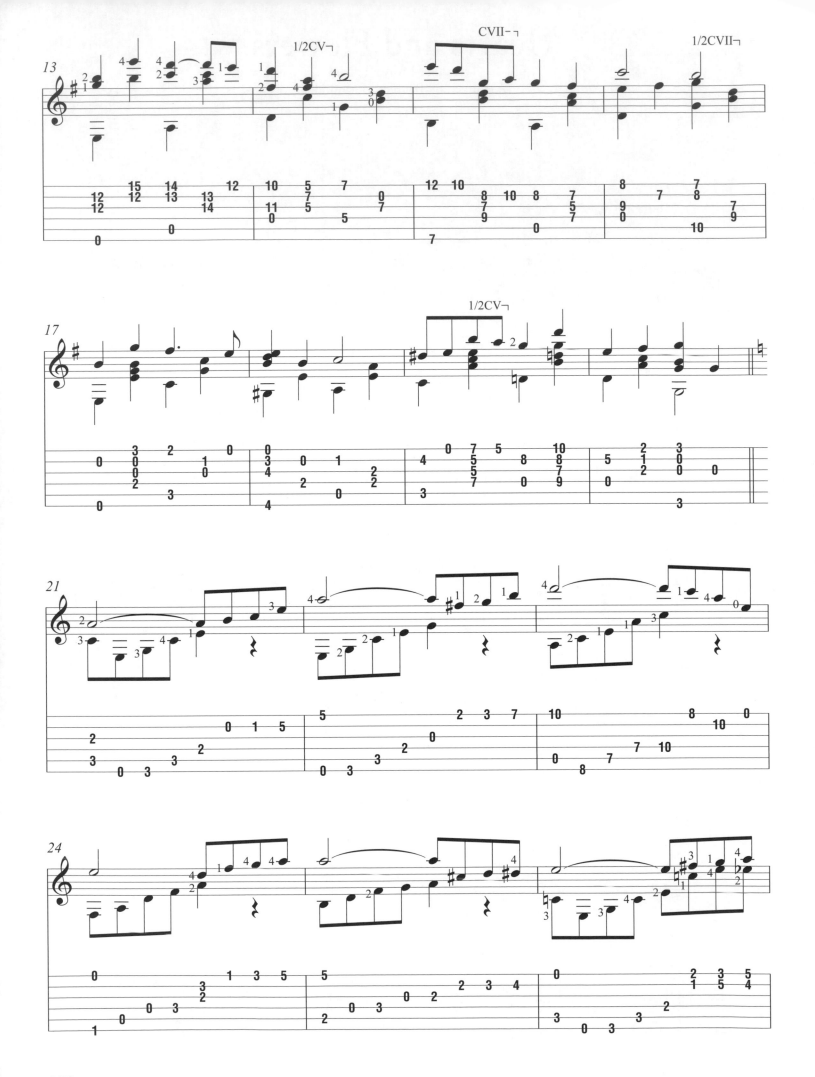

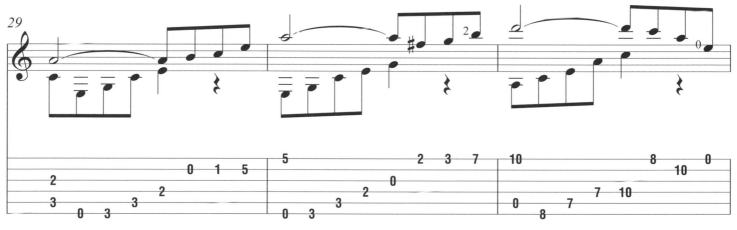

Harm.

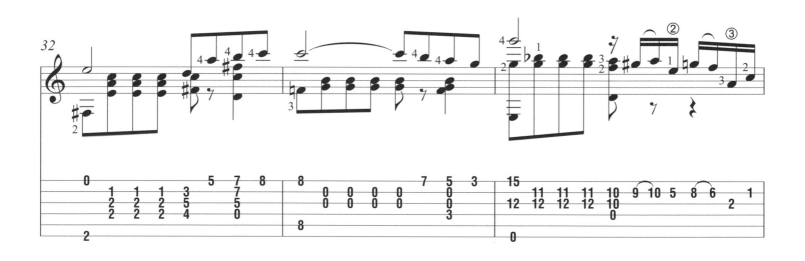

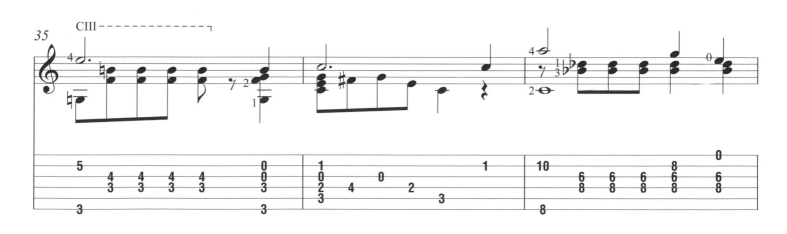

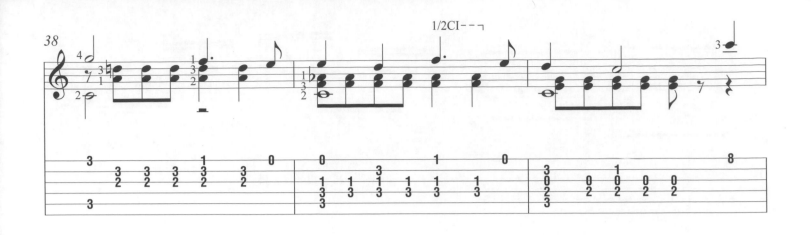

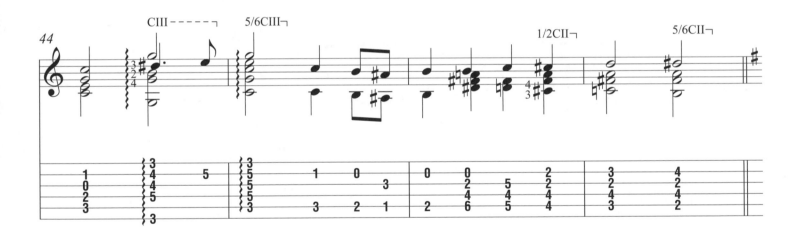

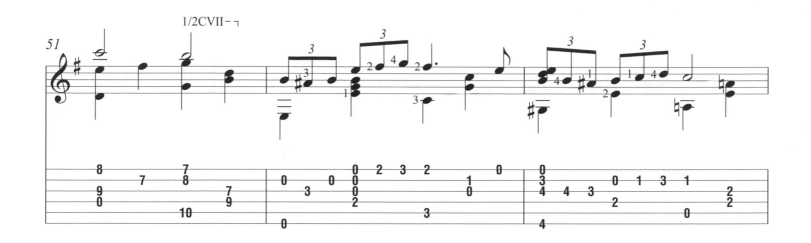

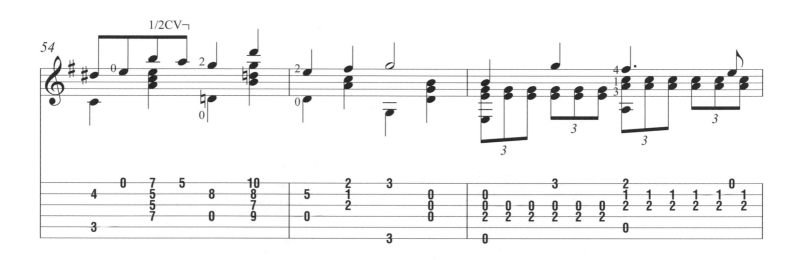

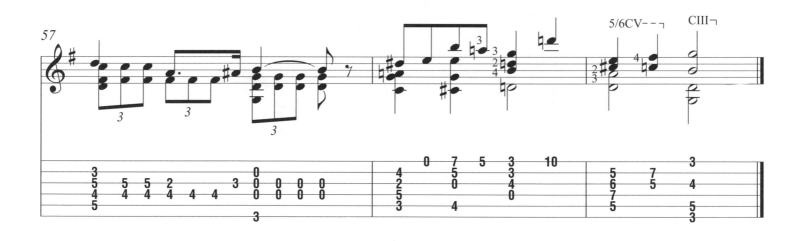

ABOUT THE AUTHOR

Bridget Mermikides (formerly Upson) grew up in a family of musicians in the Lake District of England and began playing the cello at age 6. Upon hearing a John Williams recording at age 13 she became instantly and irrecoverably smitten with the classical guitar and has devoted her life to the instrument.

A graduate of the Royal Academy of Music (where she received tuition from John Williams and Julian Bream), Bridget now teaches and performs as a soloist and ensemble player and writes a monthly column for *Guitar Techniques Magazine*. She is the author of two previous books; *The Classical Guitar Compendium* and *The Classical Guitar Anthology* (both published by Hal Leonard). Bridget lives in London with her husband and daughter.

www.bridgetmermikides.com

HAL LEONARD
CLASSICAL GUITAR METHOD

ALSO AVAILABLE

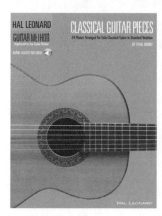

CLASSICAL GUITAR PIECES
24 Pieces Arranged for Solo Guitar in Standard Notation
BY PAUL HENRY

A great supplement to the *Hal Leonard Classical Guitar Method*, this songbook with online audio features 24 pieces ideal for students to play, including: Allegretto (Fernando Carulli) • Allegro (Wolfgang Mozart) • Andante (Matteo Carcassi) • Andante in C (Fernando Sor) • Estudio (Fernando Sor) • Orlando Sleepeth (John Dowland) • Pastorale (Matteo Carcassi) • Simple Gifts (American Traditional) • and more. Please note this book does not include tablature. The audio is accessed online using the unique code inside each book and can be streamed or downloaded. The audio files include *PLAYBACK+*, a multi-functional audio player that allows you to slow down audio without changing pitch, set loop points, change keys, and pan left or right.

00697388 Book/Online Audio..$9.99

HAL LEONARD FLAMENCO GUITAR METHOD

Learn to Play Flamenco Guitar with Step-by-Step Lessons and Authentic Pieces to Study and Play
BY HUGH BURNS

Here's your complete guide to learning flamenco guitar! This method uses traditional Spanish flamenco song forms and classical pieces to teach you the basics of this style and technique. You'll learn to play in the style of Paco de Lucia, Sabicas, Niño Ricardo and Ramón Montoya. Lessons cover: strumming, picking and percussive techniques; arpeggios; improvisation; fingernail tips; capos; and much more. Includes flamenco history and a glossary, and both standard notation and tab. The book also includes online access to 58 professionally recorded tracks for demonstration and play-along.

00697363 Book/Online Audio..$15.99

A Beginner's Guide with Step-by-Step Instruction and Over 25 Pieces to Study and Play
BY PAUL HENRY

The *Hal Leonard Classical Guitar Method* is designed for anyone just learning to play classical guitar. This comprehensive and easy-to-use beginner's guide by renowned classical guitarist and teacher Paul Henry uses the music of the master composers to teach you the basics of the classical style and technique. The accompanying audio features all the pieces in the book for demonstration and play along. Includes pieces by Beethoven, Bach, Mozart, Schumann, Giuliani, Carcassi, Bathioli, Aguado, Tarrega, Purcell, and more. Includes all the basics plus info on PIMA technique, two- and three-part music, time signatures, key signatures, articulation, free stroke, rest stroke, composers, and much more. Does NOT include tablature. Audio is accessed online using the unique code inside each book and can be downloaded or streamed. The audio also includes *PLAYBACK+* features such as tempo adjustment, looping, and other features to assist with practice.

00697376 Book/Online Audio..$15.99

HAL LEONARD CLASSICAL GUITAR METHOD – TAB EDITION
BY PAUL HENRY

00142652 Book/Online Audio...$14.99

Prices, contents, and availability subject to change without notice.

HAL•LEONARD®
www.halleonard.com

CLASSICAL GUITAR

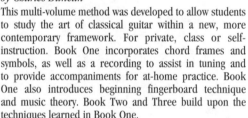